Leading

ADMINISTRATOR
CLARITY

School-Wide Strategies for Cultivating Communication, Fostering a Responsive Culture, and Inspiring Intentional Leadership

Sandy Brunet, Carin Fractor,
and Marine Freibrun

Published by:
Ulysses Press
PO Box 3440
Berkeley, CA 94703
www.ulyssespress.com

ISBN: 978-1-64604-355-2
Library of Congress Control Number: 2022932300

Printed in the United States by Versa Press
10 9 8 7 6 5 4 3 2 1

Acquisitions editor: Claire Sielaff
Managing editor: Claire Chun
Project editor: Renee Rutledge
Editor: Pat Harris
Proofreader: Kate St.Clair
Front cover design: Justin Shirley
Cover artwork: © bsd/shutterstock.com
Interior design and layout: Winnie Liu

CONTENTS

Our Intentional "Why"

The principalship is more than a post,

More than a rung on the ladder

Or a safe move toward retirement.

The principalship is a *calling*.

The principalship means charting uncharted waters,

Iterating, ideating,

Failing forward when it's easier to stay the course.

The principalship is also a balance;

When done best, it is intentional,

Planned, and purposeful.

Like the philosophers and academics before us,

We embrace our calling.

Empowered through collaboration,

Emboldened by one another,

Ready for the journey,

We lead intentionally with passion and purpose.

INTRODUCTION: THE "WHY" FOR OUR BOOK

Are we the only ones who have noticed that the vast majority of books written about school leadership are written by people who haven't actually led a school in recent times? We want to change that. Within this book, you will find tried-and-true information, resources, and actionable guidance that you can use *immediately* to increase your instructional effectiveness and lead your school intentionally with passion and purpose.

We are not here to tell you that we have all the answers or that the work is easy. We wrote this book because, as school leaders, each one of us had to figure out on our own how to operationalize best leadership practices. We each read every book by Simon Sinek; we followed Brené Brown's posts daily and could list the top ten effective practices within John Hattie's Visible Learning research. Yet, when it came to school leadership, we independently struggled with how to articulate all those ideas our mentors and leadership gurus espoused while also keeping our schools afloat.

It was not until the three of us moved into different roles in different states, experiencing the many emotions educators face today, that we connected as "thought partners"—people who challenge your thinking and provoke you to innovate. Through this connection, we collaborated, iterated, failed, and leaned into our own vulnerabilities to be the most intentional leaders we could for our organizations. Through this process, we were able to identify how clarity within our own leadership led to more success for our staff and our students.

During the past ten years, the concept of *teacher* clarity has gained increased traction and attention among educators. In his 2015 study, John Hattie found the effect size of teacher clarity on student achievement to be 0.75 (or equivalent to nearly two years' growth in one year's time). While the importance of an effective teacher in the classroom cannot be overstated, the school leader also plays a critical role in overall school performance and achievement. We argue that having clarity as a school administrator is equally as important as having clarity as a teacher.

Therefore, clarity as an administrator is authentically delivering intentional leadership. In this book, we begin by setting a working definition of intentional leadership. As you will learn, intentional leadership is the purposeful fostering of a responsive school culture. It helps school administrators understand the myriad factors that lead to the creation of a culture that focuses on process over perfection. Intentional leadership is the combination of setting clear and high expectations, encouraging accountability, and fostering safety and trust within a school. Together, these practices can set the stage for good staff to become great and great staff to become unstoppable.

We aim to provide a how-to guide to assist aspiring, new, and veteran administrators in creating a culture that fosters student achievement by diving into the following concepts: clarity of purpose, clarity of implementation, clarity of communication, and clarity of sustainability. We infuse the text with personal anecdotes and, of course, stories of epic failures. We include current research and pedagogy and a variety of easy-to-use, vetted resources to help school administrators become more intentional in their leadership and to create a road map for leading with "Administrator Clarity," a quality we define in Chapter 1.

We believe that, when taken as a whole, the information presented here can vastly improve the impact of your professional learning as well as that of the staff and students within your charge.

Chapter 1

OVERVIEW OF ADMINISTRATOR CLARITY

As we mentioned earlier, the idea of teacher clarity has been around for some time. The concept has been supported and popularized by John Hattie's work on Visible Learning. According to his research, "when teachers are clear in expectations and instructions, students learn more" (Hattie 2012, 18). It has also been said that teacher clarity is both a method and a mindset, and that its influence on student performance can result in nearly two years' growth in one year's time.

What seems to appeal to both teachers *and* students is that teacher clarity brings a level of transparency to teaching and learning. By teachers setting clear guidelines and expectations, students can know what is expected of them. When they know what is expected, they can create a pathway to succeed and measure their own progress.

We could not help but wonder: If clarity is a key contributor to student success in the learning environment, wouldn't the same likely hold true in any environment of teaching professionals?

As school leaders, we set out to explore this idea in more depth. We posed an informal survey to a set of over one hundred educators. We asked them about their experiences as teachers when they felt most effective, when they felt most supported, and when they could best "see" their efficacy.

The results were neither shocking nor revolutionary. Time and again, teachers attributed their successes with their students directly and indirectly to the attributes and expectations of their school leaders. When teachers know what success looks like at their school, they are more likely to see themselves as effective, to see their students as high achieving, and to note that their students' assessment scores are an accurate indicator of student learning and achievement.

Essentially, our survey told us that one of the best indicators of both teacher efficacy and teacher satisfaction was directly related to the qualities of the person at the helm of these schools. Here is where Administrator Clarity and intentional leadership come in.

We are referring to the degree to which a school leader is clear and intentional with their staff, clear and intentional with their students, and clear and intentional with their school community.

In this book, when we refer to Administrator Clarity, we are referring to the degree to which a school leader is clear and intentional with their staff, clear and intentional with their students, and clear and intentional with their school community.

This intentionality includes clarity about the vision for their school, clarity about expectations for their staff, clarity about the allocation of their resources, clarity about the decisiveness of their communication, and clarity about their overall professional purpose.

This book is divided into **four sections or domains:**

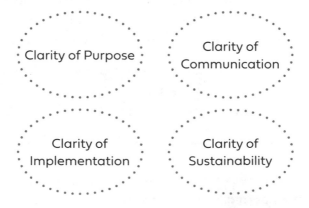

Clarity of Purpose

Clarity of Communication

Clarity of Implementation

Clarity of Sustainability

Before diving into the ideas and activities contained herein, take a moment to complete the Administrator Clarity Self-Assessment (page 125), and have your staff complete the Administrator Clarity Staff Assessment (page 129). Then use the results of these tools to draft your initial Administrator Clarity Planning Guide ().

It is important to note that the tools contained herein are *not* one-and-done activities. Truly impactful educational leaders will see this self-exploration as an iterative process. Ideally, a school

> *Truly impactful educational leaders will see this self-exploration as an iterative process.*

leader will complete this activity twice annually. We recommend that at the *very* least, these assessments are conducted annually.

Great and inspirational school leaders possess a growth mindset, and they clearly understand that their role is one of progress and not perfection. They also know that the world of education will throw curveballs their way and they can be easily distracted from growth and improvement. Therefore, we hope school leaders will build these processes into their school year calendar in the same way one would build in an important meeting. Without intentionally planning for reflection and implementing opportunities to reflect on and revise practices, it is easy to lose sight of the importance of this work. With this in mind, we created a calendar for you to refer to in utilizing the resources in this book so that you can effectively and intentionally manage your time as it relates to leading with clarity (see Sample Yearlong Plan and Template on page 38).

Before continuing further in the book, it is a good idea to become self-actualized and put on your leadership bikini. As school leaders, we ask our teachers to be transparent with their data. We push them to focus on what is within their locus of control, and we expect them to professionally manage the challenges that come when anticipated outcomes do not match actual outcomes.

This is where the metaphoric rubber meets the road, and we ask the same of you as school leaders that we ask of our teacher leaders. To truly grow in the area of Administrator Clarity, we all must begin by being honest and open with ourselves about our potential areas of strength and struggle, and we must be vulnerable and open to feedback. If our self-reflection does not match the reflections of others or we find areas of growth needed within ourselves, we must dive in and be willing to make the necessary changes to shift our course and our direction.

Reflection

After completing your self-assessment and administering your staff assessment, spend some time examining the averages of each domain. Before continuing to read the book and selecting an area of focus, think about the following questions:

- As a leader, what are your areas of strength? Why do you think these are areas of strength for you?
- What areas do both you and your staff see as areas for growth?
- In what areas is there a discrepancy between your self-assessment and the assessment of your staff? Why do you think this discrepancy may exist?

After reading each domain, reflect on two or three actionable steps you can take to begin growing in your target areas.

The Changing Role of the School Leader

We are not working in the educational landscape in which we were educated. Everyone from the superintendent to the classroom teacher is a player in the high-stakes accountability world of education. All school leaders are expected to have mastery in curriculum and assessment, high levels of budget proficiency, understanding of positive behavior support, clarity on special education laws, the ability to manage a safe facility, comprehensive knowledge of a variety of evaluation systems, amazing marketing and public relations skills, and up-to-date information on current educational mandates, laws, policies, and procedures—*and* we would love for everyone to inspire great teaching, love every student, and embody a passion and zest for lifelong learning. The

> *We are not working in the educational landscape in which we were educated. Everyone from the superintendent to the classroom teacher is a player in the high-stakes accountability world of education.*

number of different expectations of the school leader truly gives meaning to the adage "jack of all trades, master of none."

Consider the following changes in the field of education, all of which have occurred during the past decade:

- Increased systems of school-wide accountability for teachers, administrators, and students based on performance metrics
- Redefinition of the role of principal from manager to instructional leader
- Heightened awareness of a DEI (diversity, equity, and inclusion) lens that impacts student access and achievement within our schools and exacerbates opportunity gaps
- Adoption of national and state standards that increase the level of expectations for staff without increased levels of funding
- Performance-based evaluation systems

And yet we need to be a master in all of these areas.

We owe this to our teachers, we owe this to our communities, and most of all, we owe this to our students.

Gone are the days of the principal as the figurehead of the school. The new role is complex, multifaceted, and dynamic. One need look no further than the onset of the global pandemic in 2020 to be reminded of the following:

1. Education can change at any moment, and leaders must be flexible, visionary, and connected.

2. The future of education is vast, unknown, and evolving.

Although we cannot be certain what the future of education will be, we can be certain that regardless of the direction education moves in, there are core key competencies that have been proven time and again to be successful in leading brick-and-mortar schools, in leading virtual schools, and in leading hybrid schools.

Establishing a school with Administrator Clarity can be a complex and daunting process along with all of the other duties currently occupying space on a school leader's plate; it truly exemplifies the importance of spending time to save time.

> *"Clarity," when referring to the role of the school leader, means the quality of being clear, reasonable, and exact about your "what," your "why," and your "how."*

Administrator Clarity is critical in setting the culture and climate of a school because clarity increases feelings of safety, belonging, and achievement for staff, which have a direct correlation to student achievement. Leaders who employ the strategies of Administrator Clarity are experts at setting a clear and intentional purpose, employing honest and intentional communication, providing a clear system of monitoring and recognition, and employing a clear course of action, and they are clearly passionate about what they do day in and day out.

Chapter Highlights

- Administrator Clarity is defined as the degree to which a school leader is clear and intentional with their staff, clear and intentional with their students, and clear and intentional with their school community.

- Administrator Clarity can be examined in four key areas:

  » Clarity of purpose

  » Clarity of implementation

  » Clarity of communication

  » Clarity of sustainability

- Truly working on these areas requires intentionally planning for reflection and implementing opportunities to reflect and revise practices; a leader who is not strategic in planning finds it easy to become bogged down with all the other aspects of the job.

- Leading with Administrator Clarity supports school leaders in leading with intention and alignment; it eliminates confusion that staff may experience when objectives and expectations are not clear.

Chapter 2

THE RESEARCH: HOW IMPORTANT IS THE SCHOOL LEADER, REALLY?

In February 2021, the Wallace Foundation published a research report, "How Principals Affect Students and Schools: A Systematic Synthesis of Two Decades of Research," that revealed some critical findings about the importance and impact of the role of the school principal. The researchers, from Vanderbilt University, North Carolina State University, and the University of North Carolina at Chapel Hill, determined that the impact of an effective principal on a school's performance is much greater than previously believed. Specifically, school leaders had the single greatest impact on student achievement, teacher satisfaction and retention, student attendance, and reductions in exclusionary discipline. The researchers identified four principal practices that are linked to effective outcomes (Grissom, Egalite, and Lindsay 2021). They are as follows:

1. Engaging in high-leverage instructional activities

2. Building a productive school culture and climate

3. Facilitating collaboration and learning communities

4. Managing personnel and resources strategically

As we dive into our domains of Administrator Clarity, you will find that we refer back to these key practices and include tools to operationalize their impact.

The research clearly found that for improving the school as a whole, the effectiveness of the principal is more important than the effectiveness of any single teacher. It can no longer be disputed that a principal is simply a figurehead or "just" an instructional leader. It is now clear that if a school district wants to invest in improving the performance of the school as a whole, it will likely benefit from investing in one key adult in a school building, the principal. This investment alone is likely to be the most efficient way to positively impact student achievement.

In another landmark study, the University of Chicago Consortium on School Research used data from hundreds of schools to learn how principals were most effective in achieving learning gains on standardized tests (Allensworth and Hart 2018). This thorough study concluded that "principals influence school achievement primarily in changes through the school climate" (1).

According to this study, principals' effects on student achievement are mostly indirect, coming largely through their efforts to recruit, develop, support, and retain a talented teaching staff and create conditions for them to deliver strong instruction.

We would take this one step further and propose that staff are developed, are retained, and have their worth best reinforced by school leaders who are intentional and utilize the specific skills of Administrator Clarity outlined in this book.

Another important support for the role of clarity in the principalship can be found in findings by Louis et al. (2010). Their original premise was that leadership was second only to classroom instruction in terms of impact on school improvement. After completing their research, they were even more confident about this claim. According to the researchers, they did not find a single case of a school improving its student achievement record in the *absence* of talented leadership. Why is leadership crucial? One explanation is that leaders have the potential to unleash latent capacities in organizations (Louis et al. 2010, 9).

The researchers offered a definition of leadership that was distilled from the essence of their findings: "Leadership is all about organizational improvement; more specifically, it is about establishing agreed-upon and worthwhile directions for the organization in question, and doing whatever it takes to prod and support people to move in those directions" (pp. 9–10).

This research serves to further underscore and validate the premise of this book: leaders establish direction, and that direction unleashes the talent needed to push a school forward. That direction cannot exist without clarity, purpose, and intention within the mind and actions of the leader.

It is important to note that during the past decade there has been a huge push for school principals to be "instructional leaders." Nevertheless, numerous recent studies have explored how school principals must continue to balance this role with other roles they hold. This is where we believe leading with clarity and intentionality is crucial for success.

In a study of Florida principals, Horng, Lai, Klasik, and Loeb (2010) found that on average, principals spent less than 10 percent of their time on functions traditionally defined as instruction (such as classroom observations and professional development for teachers). Almost 30 percent of their time was spent on administrative activities, including student supervision, scheduling, and compliance issues; about 20 percent of their time was spent on "organizational management."

In addition, the researchers found that more time devoted to organizational management was correlated with higher student achievement as reflected by test scores. Interestingly, this study also found that the amount of time spent on instructional activities was not related or was only minimally related to student performance.

On their face, these results seem to undermine the argument that the principal is the instructional leader of a school. However, it is important to first look at the types of activities—such as ensuring that the school is safe, managing the budget and other resources, and dealing with concerns from teachers—included in organizational management. Effectively addressing such concerns provides staff members and students with a well-organized, learning-focused environment in which to work. These recent findings do not contradict the body of research arguing for principals as instructional leaders, but this new evidence does work to broaden the definition of instructional leadership to include organizational management skills (Rice 2010, 3).

Grissom and Loeb (2011) conducted a similar study that would support Rice's assessment: principals devote significant time and energy to become instructional leaders in their schools, and they are unlikely to see improvement unless they increase their capacity for organizational management as well. The overall takeaway is that "effective instructional leadership combines an understanding of the instructional needs of the school with an ability to target resources where they are needed, hire the best available teachers, provide teachers with the opportunities they need to improve, and keep the school running smoothly" (p. 32).

Effective principals agree with this assessment. Blase, Blase, and Phillips (2010) interviewed twenty principals who had been recognized by their state departments of education as high-performing principals of high-performing or significantly improving schools. These principals indicated that effective administrative leadership provides a stable, predictable, and supportive foundation for a high-performing school with intertwined and interdependent processes.

As leaders who employ Administrator Clarity, we felt it was important to outline the research because it supports the structures and coaching we provide in this book. It is also important to note that nothing in this book is revolutionary. We did not invent a new way to lead a school. We would actually argue that this would be an impossible feat.

We see this book as more of a coaching companion to a new and ever-changing face of school leadership. In essence, we feel that our research can be summarized in two final key points that have guided our work and our passions. It is critical that school leaders truly own and embrace the two main conclusions of the research. The first conclusion is as follows:

"Leadership is second only to classroom instruction among all school-related factors that contribute to what students learn at school" (Leithwood et al. 2004, 5).

This quote holds critical and monumental importance when it comes to the beliefs that we hold as school leaders. We have often been taught and led to believe that our impacts are indirect and, although they are important for the culture of the school, they have limited or minimal impact on student learning. As school leaders, it is time we debunk that long-held myth and remind ourselves that our actions, our leadership, and our clarity are critical.

The second conclusion is summed up in the following quotation:

> "Replacing a principal at the 25th percentile in effectiveness with one at the 75th percentile can increase annual student learning in math and reading by almost three months, annually" (Grissom, Egalite, and Lindsay 2021, 4).

As a profession and as a nation, we have *vastly* understated the degree to which school leadership matters and directly impacts student achievement. When we couple that understatement with the evolution of our profession over the past decade, it is evident that we need to dig into the way we view ourselves and our role as school leaders and place our own intentional leadership at the forefront of all that we do and in every way that we serve.

Chapter Highlights

- Administrator Clarity is defined as the degree to which a school leader is clear and intentional with staff, students, and the school community.
- School leadership matters: "Leadership is second only to classroom instruction among all school-related factors that contribute to what students learn at school" (Leithwood et al. 2004, 5).

Clarity of Purpose

Chapter 3

WHAT'S YOUR "WHY"?

This chapter delves into the importance of understanding why we do what we do in school leadership. It takes administrators through a series of activities that they can complete independently and in collaboration with their school leadership teams and staff, in order to determine what they believe and what their shared set of beliefs are when it comes to schools, student achievement, and leadership of learning. When you lead with clarity of purpose, your actions and outcomes are focused and impactful and align with the culture you strive to create and sustain.

Have you ever walked onto a school campus and just felt the culture? Maybe it was noticing the student art hanging in the halls, listening to the teachers deliver lessons, or hearing the chatter of the students throughout the day. When you see and hear things that foster positivity and inspiration, you know teachers and staff at a school have a shared "why" or purpose for being.

In contrast, you can also feel the negativity and pressure of school culture. When manipulation and fear take hold of the school culture, they change the trajectory of student achievement and can leave teacher and staff morale at an all-time low. There is no shared "why."

So, what is your "why" as a school leader? Do you share your mission through inspiring and valuing those who you lead?

Let's take a look at experiences from School A and School B and reflect on how these examples relate to your own experiences.

SCHOOL A

After a few years of teaching and taking some time to be at home with her young children, a novice teacher joined the staff at School A. Not knowing the culture or the administrators that well, Mrs. Novice did her best to follow school expectations and collaborate with her grade-level team. Her administrators were also new to the school and were starting out as a new team in their first years as principal and assistant principal. It did not take long for these administrators to communicate their goals to their staff, but most important, these two leaders were intentional in creating a positive school culture by establishing relationships, seeking out teacher leaders on the campus, and soliciting feedback to improve their school and their leadership of the school.

Mrs. Novice knew her administrators were being intentional in their pursuit to build relationships. When they walked through classrooms, they left simple, positive notes of feedback and praise. They recognized the great things they saw in the classrooms and valued the teachers' hard work. When teachers had formal evaluations, the feedback they received was effective and actionable—and built upon their strengths.

One of the most telling signs of this administrative team's intentional actions to build a positive school culture was the way they interacted with teachers, staff, parents, and students who walked through the campus each day. Everyone was greeted with a smile, and this administrative team knew people by name. There were clear actions made to acknowledge students' positive behavior choices, and the small talk in the hallways after school let teachers know that the admin team was truly listening to both teachers' and staff members' stories about their families and experiences.

Being brand-new to the school, Mrs. Novice did not initially seek out opportunities to become overly involved. She stayed in her classroom, taught the standards, loved her students, and provided extraordinary instruction. Then something happened.

As the administrative team visited her room more and more, they began to discover that Mrs. Novice had tremendous educational capacity and knowledge. While many other school leaders would have waited for Mrs. Novice to step into a leadership role, this administrative team did not. They recognized talent and immediately began to bring her into their discussions and listen to her ideas in order to drive the school forward.

The administrators at this school lived their "why" and purpose through their actions and clearly communicated that with the school community through intentional leadership. Their "why" permeated the hallways, and you could feel the comradery among staff and students. It was authentic, and you knew that people genuinely cared.

Unfortunately, just as you can have that feeling of excitement and positivity, you can also sense a feeling of dread and doom on a school campus.

SCHOOL B

Since Mrs. Novice knew what it was like to be at a positive and uplifting school, the feeling of negativity was evident when she started at a new school site several years later. It did not take long for Mrs. Novice to develop anxiety as she worked at this new school. It was not so much that there was an absence of student work or artwork displayed; it was the way students were treated in the hallways and how staff and teachers were addressed by the administration. When administrators entered the room for informal observations, no notes were left, and feedback on instructional delivery and impact was not given. Instead, negative emails were sent about student behavior. Positive strategies or actions were not recognized. Even worse, instructional coaches had the power to stop lessons as they walked through and take over the teaching. The self-efficacy of teachers like Mrs. Novice slowly diminished as the school year went on.

Mrs. Novice, now having many years of teaching under her belt and being both highly skilled and nationally recognized for her contributions to education, scheduled a meeting with her school leadership. Her hope was to assist them in understanding her challenges at the school site and offer her perspective and time to help improve school morale, student achievement, and implementation of restorative practices. She made detailed notes for the meeting. Her offers of support and her feelings were dismissed. She went into that meeting with the whole purpose of proposing possible solutions for improving the school and left the meeting with the determination to find a new job. While the school would have greatly benefited from at least hearing this perspective, which was also shared by many of Mrs. Novice's colleagues, ego got in the way and the school lost a legendary teacher because of the hubris of the school leadership.

While we all hope for a school culture similar to that of School A, leaders must be reflective and ask themselves if their current culture is representative of their purpose and passion for leading. Does your school culture articulate your "why"?

When we think about our "why" as administrators, we might think about our school's performance on the end-of-year summative state assessment. But our "why" is not about that test. The test is *what* we do at the end to measure student learning. Our teachers and staff are not going to buy into students doing well on the test simply because that is "what we do." They are going to be loyal and inspired when they know *why* we do it.

So, let's start with reflecting on our "why."

What is your purpose as a school leader? In his book, *Start with Why* (Sinek 2011), Sinek describes thinking about our "why" through a series of questions:

- What is your purpose, cause, or belief?
- Why does your organization exist?
- Why do you get out of bed every morning?
- Why should anyone care?

If you take the time to really answer those questions, they will guide you in thinking about your purpose and the clarity and intentionality of your actions as a school leader. (See the Articulating Your "Why" activity on page 133.)

Let's take Ms. Perez's experience as a teacher at school. Her administrators set out their purpose as school leaders at the start of the school year by explaining their individual purposes, why their school exists, what drove them to get out of bed every morning, and why teachers and staff at the school should care. Ms. Perez's administrators presented their own "whys" to their staff, sharing pictures of their families, their journeys to school leadership, and what their expectations were for the school. After sharing their purpose and reason for coming to school every day, they asked staff members to think about their own purpose. Teachers were asked to reflect quietly on their own purpose. The principal modeled for her staff and shared that her purpose was to ensure high expectations and academic rigor for all students because she grew up in a low-income area where it was expected that she would not achieve. It was important to Ms. Perez's administrator to empower all students. After listening to their administrator take down her armor and be vulnerable in front of her staff, teachers were more willing to be vulnerable themselves and write down their thoughts; if they felt comfortable, they could share their ideas with their colleagues. The administrators guided Ms. Perez and the rest of the staff through answering the next series of questions.

- Why does our school exist?
- Why do you get out of bed every morning?
- Why should anyone care?

With every question, the principal and assistant principal shared their answers, along with stories. Ms. Perez engaged in meaningful conversations with her colleagues during that staff meeting and was able to make connections with her administrators while also being able to understand them on a different level. The administrators' sharing of this process with their staff was an important part of building a positive culture while also demonstrating to the staff that the administrators had a goal, a reason, and ultimately a "why" behind their plan for the school.

There was a huge difference in the "whys" for School A and School B. While we understand that no one wakes up wanting to lead a culture similar to that described in School B, we all have had times when we disconnected from our purpose and then recognized that our interactions with those we served were antithetical to what drove us to lead and educate in the first place. While examining Table 3.1, reflect on what type of school you currently lead. Does it fall within the description of only School A or School B?

"Why"	School A	School B
What is your purpose, cause, or belief?	To empower staff, students, and families as learners within the school community.	To find deficits and negativity in the data.
Why does your school exist?	To ensure staff, students, and families feel valued within the community and add value back to the community.	To blame teachers for ineffective instructional practices.
Why do you get out of bed every morning?	To inspire others to take risks in their learning.	To do the things we've always done because that's what we've always done.
Why should anyone care?	They care because their role in the community matters each and every day in the lives of the students whom they serve.	No one cares—just add more work.

Table 3.1. Developing Your "Why"

The truth is that leading with your "why" falls on a continuum, and we move along that continuum in both directions yearly, monthly, and sometimes even daily. We will always feel that gravitational pull away from our core, and thus we must be intentional and clear in what we believe and what drives the work we do day in and day out in order to lead our schools in a manner that aligns with our "why."

I Understand My "Why,"
but How Do I Live It?

Intentionally leading through your purpose and beliefs falls into the second ring of Simon Sinek's famed Golden Circle. Sinek explains that your "how" is defined by your "values or principles that bring your cause to life," and it helps you implement and live your "why."

> "In order to improve HOW and WHAT we do, we constantly look to what others are doing. We attend conferences, read books, talk to friends and colleagues to get their input and advice, and sometimes we are also the dispensers of advice. We are in pursuit of understanding the best practices of others to help guide us. But it is a flawed assumption that what works for one organization will work for another. Even if the industries, sizes and market conditions are the same, the notion that 'if it's good for them, it's good for us' is simply not true" (Sinek 2011, 12).

> "We say WHAT we do, we sometimes say HOW we do it, but we rarely say WHY we do WHAT we do" (Sinek 20011, 69).

Your "how" is what helps you hold your teachers and staff accountable to understanding and achieving the school's collective vision (more on this in Chapter 4). When you are clear in *how* you do things within your organization, you will also attract people with shared beliefs and a collective mission, helping your organization thrive naturally.

Let's take School A, for example.

The staff's collective mission was to provide all learners with an enriching education. They were there because they wanted everyone to feel safe, valued, and loved, which drove their desire to go to school day in and day out. They felt people should care about the cause because they collectively cared about their students' personal and academic progress and success.

So, *how* did the staff at School A arrive at their collective belief and mission? This is where leading with Administrator Clarity really comes in. When the administrators of School A *collaboratively developed and communicated* their "whys" and invited teachers and staff to participate in this process, this joint contribution led to a collective school culture with a committed focus on students' growth and well-being.

We have compiled some strategies in the Reflective, Physical, Personal, and Instructional Communication worksheets and resources in the appendix to help you and your staff begin to not only articulate your "why" but also communicate it.

Chapter Highlights

- Articulating your "why" is imperative for leading with clarity.
- Your "why" should be felt throughout your school.
- Some activities to collectively develop your "why" with staff include the following:

  » Reflective communication

  » Physical communication

  » Personal communication

  » Instructional communication

Chapter 4

USING YOUR "WHY" TO SET YOUR MISSION AND VISION

It is essential for all school leaders, new and veteran, to examine their belief systems and purpose for leading and ensure that there is value alignment between their "why" and the mission and vision of the organization. This chapter provides simple, straightforward, and engaging ways for school administrators to walk their staff through creating a vision and mission that align with the collective "why" of the organization.

Once you have developed your "why" and given your staff the opportunity to think and cultivate their own "whys," it is time to put it into action. This is where creating a clear mission, vision, and set of core values comes into play.

Clarifying Your Mission

While your "why" statement gets you out of bed each day, your mission defines what you are working toward. It establishes the framework for the *behavior* of each and every member of your school, ultimately guiding goals and decision-making.

When you are developing a mission for your school, it is imperative to involve everyone in the process. A mission is the collective responsibility of all those involved in ensuring that students are learning, and thus everyone should play a role in the development process.

With your "why" statement at the forefront, think about what factors set the stage as you develop your mission statement. Are you affected by teacher turnover or the need to close the achievement gap? Is there a push for professional growth or to gain teacher buy-in? Does your school need a change in attitude or in setting the stage? Is there population growth or decline? Are you framing your vision around diversity, equity, and inclusion?

Now for crafting our statements.

As you work with your staff to define the mission statement, think about the following:

- Which of your staff's duties, actions, and behaviors align with your "why"?
- What inspires your day-to-day activities within the school?

Staff Mission Statement Activity

This activity was developed for new school leaders, or school leaders who need to revisit their "why" to work with the school staff and to develop clarity around the mission statement. As we shared in our example, it is critical to develop shared buy-in among staff members, and this activity can help.

1. Form teams of teachers (mixing up the grade levels and content areas works best). Give the team members paper and three minutes to write a statement to answer the question "What is the purpose of our school?" Instruct them not to put their name on their paper and to write legibly, skipping lines.

2. Each team member then passes the statement to the person on the right. That person underlines the significant passages or words and then passes the paper to the next person. Team members continue to pass and underline until everyone gets their own statement back. It is acceptable to have multiple underlines under key phrases.

3. A recorder then writes all of the underlined statements on a piece of chart paper so everyone can read them.

4. Each team generates one mission statement based on the underlined statements.

   a. Does the mission statement take into account all or most of the items listed?

   b. Does it focus on the ones the team has the most agreement on (most underlined)?

During a subsequent meeting, provide each team of teachers with a list of the previous team-generated mission statements. Have the teams read through the list and consolidate the items into three mission statements, ultimately identifying one that they believe encompasses the core values of the organization.

Teams can then present their singular mission statements, and collectively the staff should come to consensus on one statement that they feel represents the collective core values and the school's purpose for existing—the driving force behind the work they do on a daily basis.

Moving from Mission to Vision

According to Frank Slide in his article, "What Are the Five Performance Objectives of Operations Management," a **vision** is "a vivid mental image of what you want your school to be at some point in the future, based on your goals and aspirations. A vision statement captures, in writing, the essence of where you want to take your school, and it can inspire you and your staff to reach your goals. Vision statements are often not fully attainable, yet they create a shared purpose to work toward."

Think about these questions when drafting your vision:

- What are your hopes?
- What problem are you solving?
- Who and what are you aspiring to change?

Let's think about your vision statement.

The goal of the vision statement is to give teachers and staff members an idea of what your school hopes to accomplish collaboratively. It is not necessarily an effective way to drive an individual's behavior or expectations for day-to-day activities, but it sets the bar high for the daily actions that take place within the school. The vision statement encourages growth, both internally and externally.

Here is a quick activity that you can do with your staff to help develop a vision statement, a six-word story.

Creating a Vision Activity—Six-Word Story

Have each person on your staff take out a sticky note, and ask them these questions:

- What are your hopes?
- What problem are you solving?
- Who and what are you aspiring to change?

Ask them to think about words that come to mind when they think about those things.

Have them write down those words on the sticky notes.

Have them choose only *six* words from their list.

They can move punctuation around, add figurative language, and then reread for purpose.

Sometimes schools use mission and vision statements interchangeably. It is important to develop both of these with your staff members because they are interdependent. Both purpose (mission) and meaning (vision) are critical for success.

Table 4.1 offers several examples of schools' vision and mission statements. Note the clear difference between the vision and mission statements for each school.

Mission	Vision
Concentrates on the present	Focuses on the future
Answers the question "Why do we exist?"	Answers the question "In a perfect world, and an idealized state, where do we want to be?"
Defines the organization's goals, ethics, and/or culture	Describes a brighter future, instills hope, and aligns with the organization's values and culture
Comes from the mind	Comes from the heart
Sets clarity and direction	Is aspirational
Inspires action	Inspires dreams

Table 4.1. Mission versus Vision

Living Your Mission and Vision through Your Core Values

The core values of an organization are those values we hold within us. They form the foundation on which we perform our daily work and conduct ourselves. Core values support how we interact with one another and are part of the strategies we use to fulfill our mission and vision. They are the basic elements of how we go about our work in everything we do.

To identify your own personal core values or the collective core values of your organization, start by describing the work you do in the form of nouns. *What keywords are at the core of your daily work with teachers, staff, and students and their families?*

For example, does the work you do center on collaboration, perseverance, and curiosity? If so, your core values may include words such as "professionalism," "teamwork," and "integrity." Whatever they are, be sure there is alignment with your "why," your mission, and your vision.

When the three of us (Sandy, Carin, and Marine) met to discuss our blog, *The Intentional Principal*, we focused not on the content we wanted to produce but on what defined our mission and vision. We started off by listing nouns that defined who we were at our core. We then took those nouns (e.g., "authenticity," "servant leader," "flexibility") and elaborated on them to ultimately develop the intentional principal core values in Table 4.2. These values drove the content we put out and the daily work we did within our school buildings.

Value	Descriptor
We are authentic.	We are intentional in our message. We are transparent, compassionate, and self-reflective. We strive to be the most true and honest version of ourselves when we lead.
We care more about doing right than being right.	We are intentional in our impact-based decision-making. We place doing what is right above all else. We are strategic and explicit in our implementation, and we let a just cause be our driver.
We serve others.	We are intentional in empowering each member of our team to build capacity among those around us. We strive to create a legacy of leaders with the belief that we are only as strong as our weakest link.
We listen more than we speak.	We are intentional in our listening. We listen to understand. We pause, process, and are present to communicate to the speaker the value of their message.
We know when to pivot.	We are intentional in shifting with the waves of our dynamic profession. As educators, we understand that the minute we think it's all figured out, something will change. Nothing taught us this more clearly than the 2020 global pandemic. And so, we pivot. We are not discouraged by change. We embrace it.
We root for each other.	We intentionally create systems of support for one another. We exclaim with excitement when someone in our group succeeds, and we work to learn from them to better ourselves. We have a collectivist mindset and understand that working in cohorts, we can achieve so much more than we could when working in isolation.

Table 4.2. Intentional Principal Core Values

As you work with your staff to define the core values of your organization, walk them through the Core Values Questions on page 135 to help them narrow their focus and articulate core values that align with their personal "why" statements and with the collective mission and vision of the school. When we know our "why," we can connect that belief with our core values. Using what your staff has already done in identifying their personal "why" statements, as well as the school's collective mission and vision, will be helpful as you establish your school's core values with clarity and intentionality. We've also provided Examples of School Mission, Vision, and Core Values (page 136) to compare with your own.

Chapter Highlights

- Mission, vision, and values must align with your "why."

- Development of the mission, vision, and core values should be a collective, iterative process.

- Mission, vision, and core values should move beyond the page they are listed on and be known and felt throughout the entire organization.

SECTION 2

Clarity of Implementation

Chapter 5

CREATING AND IMPLEMENTING MEANINGFUL GOALS

This chapter provides a rationale and resources for school leaders to be intentional and clear in how they develop systems that will support the implementation and success of any school-wide plan and align it with state or federal accountability requirements. It provides specific examples and templates coupled with anecdotes and explanations that will empower you to monitor your plan in a way that is aligned with your passion and purpose *and* lead to positive student outcomes through clarity of action.

When you became a school administrator, were you taught how to manage a complex organization, including budget analysis and implementation science? Were you coached or guided in how to perform a school-wide needs assessment with multiple stakeholders, use the input from this needs assessment to create an action plan, allocate funding and align it with specific goals and actions outlined in the plan, *and* have a progress monitoring tool to know whether you were on track to meet your mark?

Yeah, neither were we!

Yet, as intentional leaders, we know these actions are imperative in student academic achievement. Grissom and Loeb (2011) found that principals who excelled in using organizational management skills to develop, implement, and monitor plans aimed at increasing student academic achievement saw a significant increase in academic growth among their students.

We have met many principals who have spent their whole career searching for tips and resources to help them make sense of the varied accountability requirements and state and federal plan and monitoring templates. However, despite the myriad handouts and workshops available, the information still seems as clear as mud.

Monitoring the Process, Not Just the Outcome

Think back to a Friday night when you came home after a long day at work. As you sat down to dinner, your family asked you how your day went. The split second before you answered, you recalled the many things that happened from the moment you stepped onto campus to the second you exited your school doors.

The days of the school leader are long and arduous, and honestly, they can be a bit hectic. On most days, we feel we are pulled in so many different directions that it is difficult to stay focused on the "right" work. And thus, we have a sense of accomplishment when we can cross something off our list and feel good about moving down to the next task.

While there are many important things we need to complete in our role, it is critical for us to focus our time and attention on the *process* of leading, rather than simply the intended *outcomes* of our leadership. Don't get us wrong—outcomes are important. We understand that. But if we spend our time focusing solely on the outcomes, we lose sight of the real work of leading with clarity, and no matter how hard we try, sometimes we will miss the mark when we do not focus on the process.

As school leaders, we all have some sort of formal accountability measures in place that we must adhere to in order to monitor the process and plan. Depending on your educational setting, if you receive state or federal funding, you will complete monitoring tools that demonstrate how you have accounted for each dollar you were allocated. You will be expected to explain how you tied those dollars to a specific action plan that will ultimately lead to student achievement. This is where *clarity of implementation* is instrumental and critical.

We can all name the many acronyms we have learned over the years that have been part of this process. We can share our headaches and the stress that has come with completing these tools, unsure when we finish whether we have actually met the mark. The requirements and mandates can be overwhelming and seem complicated. We know this from personal experience, as we have each overcomplicated this process, muddying the waters and rendering us immobile about where to even begin. Yet monitoring and accountability are not necessarily bad things. While the tools and requirements can be overwhelming, leading a responsive culture in which these plans and tools are the norm can be an important *part* of the process. If you embrace their role and harness their power, you will see how these will make your job as an intentional leader easier and allow for clarity for all stakeholders within the organization.

Let's start with the most important part. There are two constants in every school year:

- The school year does have an ending.
- We will see results in areas where we focus our time, money, and energy.

So, let's look at an example of a time when Carin implemented SMART goals and focused teachers' attention on instruction and learning during the Coronavirus pandemic.

> During the initial stages of the pandemic, our classes were completely virtual; teachers were learning how to use new online platforms while also trying to plan their lessons, engage their students, monitor learning, and communicate with the students' families. The amount of cognitive load was high—yet, as the leader of the school, I knew we still needed to ensure that we were moving forward as a professional learning community. Our team had started this journey about three years prior to the start of the pandemic, and we were making steady progress. I knew we needed to stay focused and keep moving forward on our journey despite the challenges we faced. Our students needed us to keep their learning needs at the forefront, especially now. I

wondered how I could ask my staff to add another item to their already full plate and still meet the needs of our students.

What we ultimately decided was to be impactful in a small, manageable way. We focused on creating grade-level specific, measurable, attainable, relevant, and time-bound (SMART) goals in short cycles, one goal at a time. We created assessments as teams, planned instruction, provided targeted intervention to those students who needed additional time and support, and then assessed for mastery. While this process was in the initial stages, it kept our grade-level teams focused on what was within their control, focused on the skills being taught, and focused on learning. Through this process, we saw growth in learning and in skills. I knew that the staff members were exhausted and the weight of COVID-19 protocols and constant changes in schedules weighed on them, but I also noticed that the data was energizing for them. Their determined focus on short, formative assessments and the learning of specific skills and targets allowed our staff to visibly see the impact they had on student academic growth. Though we focused on small goals, one by one, it was their intentional focus that made a huge difference in student learning.

This story is nothing groundbreaking. Yet it highlights the idea that initiating a cycle of improvement in a small way with intention and clarity *can* yield results. The question we always get is "Where do I begin? Where is my entry point?" To be honest, we suggest starting anywhere. Just start. There is no perfect entry point to begin this work, but we have tools for each step along the way. Pick up where you feel comfortable initiating the process.

Step 1: Start with the End in Mind, and Use Data as Your Guide

What is the goal for your students this year? If students have experienced unfinished learning because of the pandemic, what areas of growth does your school need to focus on in order to achieve results for students in their future learning? What skills can you leverage so students have the requisite content knowledge to be successful next year?

What does your school-wide data tell you about student achievement? Are there systemic barriers that are disproportionately impacting specific groups of students? Do not gloss over your data. Take a deep dive. Drill your data down.

You can also determine school-wide goals by utilizing a needs assessment. Many protocols for analyzing data and determining your area of focus can be found online. We are partial to using the Sample Needs Assessment on page 137 to guide our analysis of data to determine needs and focus areas for growth within a year.

As a reminder, keep it simple! There is no perfect science to identify where to begin and what goals to generate. However, there are important things to consider:

1. Do the goals impact student academic and personal achievement and growth? If the answer is no, keep looking. You need to pare down to the most critical needs if you want to have true Administrator Clarity.

2. Are the goals specific, measurable, attainable, relevant, and time-bound? Get where we are going here? Yes—our goals must hit the mark on every letter in our SMART acronym. Otherwise, what's the purpose?

3. Are the goals aligned with your organization's goals? Be sure that your goals connect with your district or organizational mission and vision.

Step 2: Articulate the Goals to Everyone

Goals for the sake of checking an accountability box are meaningless. You will hear us mention this often. Goals have a purpose, and when they are developed intentionally and communicated with those involved, the results can be transformative. Sharing school-wide goals not only increases accountability but also generates a wider range of collective responsibility.

With that, we say *communicate*! Your goals need to be shared with anyone involved—this includes teachers, school staff, parents, district employees, *and* students! Often, we input our school-wide goals on forms, have them approved by a representative group of stakeholders, and then revisit them at the end of the year. We are here to tell you that is not enough. *Everyone needs to know the goals, live the goals, and feel connected to the goals.*

Your three to five school-wide goals *need* to be communicated and revisited at least every twelve weeks, first by your leadership team and then by the entire staff. Teachers may roll their eyes at your request to hear about their progress toward the goals, but they will never question your purpose or feel there is a lack of clarity in what you are looking for as their leader.

Do not overcomplicate this process. Table 5.1 shows some quick and easy ways to communicate your goals with everyone throughout the year.

Communication Purpose and Frequency

Weekly	Keep your school-wide goals at the top of every school site meeting agenda.
Monthly	Highlight the goals in your newsletter to the school community. (Summarize the rationale for the goals based on the needs assessment—in other words, share your data! Transparency is critical.)
Monthly	Highlight the goals in your staff newsletter. It's a great idea to have a section showcasing the area of focus at the top of the newsletter.
Monthly	Highlight which goals are being addressed in your yearlong school improvement plan and how you are allocating resources and professional development aligned with these goals.
Quarterly	Share progress toward goals with everyone involved.
Annually	Share the summary of results for all goals.

Table 5.1. Ways to Communicate School Goals with Stakeholders

Step 3: Create the Plan

This step often gets overlooked yet is important for the success of student achievement. While this task may seem overwhelming, we are going to take you back to our first step—start with the end in mind. Your goals should drive your yearlong planning and actions. Every staff meeting, collaborative planning time, and extended day time should be intentionally planned out to align with the goals.

The sense of urgency to increase student achievement should be palpable throughout your hallways. We no longer have time to throw spaghetti on the wall and wait to see what sticks. We need an action plan, and we need it to work now. Our students are relying on us to plan out specific, evidence-based actions that will lead to their success.

While you can find thousands of strategies and actions to add to your plan upon a quick internet search, no school leader we know has time to vet these and start from scratch. Work smarter, not harder, and leverage your resources.

Ask yourself—What strategies are going to be an integral part of our system? Is it worth spending money and time on a strategy that can increase writing proficiency? Maybe.

Think systematic and think long-lasting. We strongly believe that as long as you have a data system that can give you immediate feedback on formative and summative assessments and the data is arranged in a manner in which teachers can pinpoint specific target areas that were met or not met and have student names attached to those areas, you can lead the way to the finale.

Instead of being distracted by the shiny new program, try our suggestion for making systematic improvement. It can be added to any plan aimed at increasing student achievement. If you do not know where to begin, start with these foundational components:

- Learning targets identified (essential skills and priority standards)
- Common formative assessments created
- Content taught through evidenced-based strategies

- Common formative assessments administered
- Data analyzed
- Targeted interventions and extensions implemented

Examine your goals. What are the actions required to reach them? Your leadership should take your staff through the previously mentioned learning cycles through the lens of your goals.

If you want to increase reading comprehension of informational text across all grade levels, then your SMART goals should focus on the learning progressions and prerequisites required to meet those specific content skills. If you want to increase mathematical reasoning, the same holds true.

Table 5.2 provides a sample yearlong plan and template as a model for planning the learning cycles and professional development for your teaching staff with your school-wide goals in mind.

Staff Meetings	Professional Learning Community (PLC) Time
AUGUST	
• Establish mission, vision, and values • Define a team—coordination versus collaboration • Create norms, agendas, and protocols • Analyze school-wide data and develop goals	• Identify norms and agenda template • Analyze grade-level data • Identify first SMART goals for grade level
SEPTEMBER	
• Model how to design a common formative assessment (CFA) aligned with SMART goals • Provide time for teams to create pre/post CFAs • Identify dates for pre/post CFAs	• Have teams create pre/post CFAs aligned with SMART goals • Have teams identify dates for pre/post CFAs

Staff Meetings	Professional Learning Community (PLC) Time
OCTOBER	
• Model use of data analysis protocol for CFAs • Provide time for teams to use data analysis protocol • *Celebrate successes* (adult and student) • Identify students who need more time and support with SMART goal • Create a plan for these students to meet SMART goal	• Analyze CFAs using data analysis protocol • *Celebrate successes* (adult and student) • Identify students who need more time and support with SMART goal • Create a plan for these students to meet SMART goal
NOVEMBER	
• Provide time for teams to create new SMART goals • Provide time for teams to create pre/post CFAs aligned with SMART goals **Thanksgiving Break**	• Create new SMART goals • Create pre/post CFAs aligned with SMART goals • Identify dates for pre/post CFAs
DECEMBER	
• Review PLC pathway and progress toward grade-level SMART goals as a staff • *Celebrate successes* (adult and student) • Identify students at risk of not meeting SMART goal • Provide time for teams to develop a plan to provide these students with more time and support to meet SMART goal **Winter Break**	• Have teams self-assess where they are on the PLC pathway • Analyze exit ticket data to check progress toward grade-level SMART goals • *Celebrate successes* (adult and student) • Identify students at risk of not meeting SMART goal • Develop a plan to provide these students with more time and support to meet SMART goal

Staff Meetings	Professional Learning Community (PLC) Time
JANUARY/FEBRUARY	
• Review mission, vision, and values • Review PLC pathway as a school • Model use of data analysis protocol for CFAs • Provide time for teams to use data analysis protocol • *Celebrate successes* (adult and student) • Provide time for teams to identify students who need more time and support with SMART goal • Provide time for teams to create a plan for these students to meet SMART goal	• Use data analysis protocol to review results of CFAs and develop action plan for students not meeting SMART goal • *Celebrate successes* (adult and student) • Identify students who need more time and support with SMART goal • Create a plan for these students to meet SMART goal
MARCH	
• Provide time for teams to create new SMART goals • Provide time for teams to create pre/post CFAs aligned with SMART goals	• Create new SMART goals • Create pre/post CFAs aligned with SMART goals • Identify dates for pre/post CFAs
APRIL	
• Provide time for teams to use data analysis protocol • *Celebrate successes* (adult and student) • Provide time for teams to identify students who need more time and support with SMART goal • Provide time for teams to create a plan for these students to meet SMART goal **Spring Break**	• Use data analysis protocol to review results of CFAs and develop action plan for students not meeting SMART goal • *Celebrate successes* (adult and student) • Identify students who need more time and support with SMART goal • Create a plan for these students to meet SMART goal

Staff Meetings	Professional Learning Community (PLC) Time
MAY	
• Provide time for teams to create new SMART goals • Provide time for teams to create pre/post CFAs aligned with SMART goals	• Create new SMART goals • Create pre/post CFA aligned with SMART goals • Identify dates for pre/post CFAs
JUNE	
• Provide time for teams to use data analysis protocol • Provide time for teams to identify students who need more time and support with SMART goal • Provide time for teams to create a plan for these students to meet SMART goal • *Celebrate successes* (adult and student)	• Use data analysis protocol to review results of CFAs and develop action plan for students not meeting SMART goal • Identify students who need more time and support with SMART goal • Create a plan for these students to meet SMART goal • *Celebrate successes* (adult and student)

Table 5.2. Sample Yearlong Plan and Template

Step 4: Implement the Plan and Lead

Now that you have a clear path toward your goal, the fun begins! This is the heart of the work we do to impact student learning. Your role as a school leader during this time is critical in meeting your school-wide goals.

We are currently knee-deep in a global pandemic, and no one can truly tell us how this story will end. We expect our staff to come in every single day and face all the challenges in this world, continue to press forward, and make a difference in the lives of children. Every day, they have a job to do. And so do we.

We believe in the idea that now, more than ever, teachers need ongoing professional development focused on the daily actions that they are taking to support student learning and growth. When we say "professional development," this includes coaching and time to complete the following:

- Dive into data analysis to drive instruction
- Plan out fluid interventions focused on specific target skills to create meaningful SMART goals
- Generate pre- and post-assessments to measure learning progress

We view these learning growth opportunities as something being done *for* our staff rather than *to* them.

Our teachers deserve more than just managers of contract tracing and public health protocols. Our teachers deserve someone who continues not only to celebrate them but to lead them. They need more than words of encouragement that they are amazing educators and little treats to keep up their spirits. They deserve connection to a leader who believes in and builds on their efficacy in the face of the most impossible of situations.

If you believe in your staff's collective efficacy, you need to demonstrate this in the way you intentionally plan opportunities for learning and growth professionally, even amid a pandemic and the challenges that come with it. Like their students, your teachers crave and long for their pre-COVID lives, yet we cannot predict when this will all end.

What you can do for your staff is provide them with unconditional support, leadership, and guidance. As we hear stories of principals who are stepping back their expectations and the time they spend with their teachers to keep their teachers from being overwhelmed, we would ask one question of you:

What's Your "Why"?

If you know the answer to this question, then you are ready to make this shift and lead forward. Again, time is a commodity, and lack of it is often the first barrier to providing a space for our teachers to do the work needed to make an impact on student learning. So, how do we leverage our time to align with our school-wide goals?

For starters, let us focus on your predetermined staff meeting time provided by your organization. How do you currently use that time with staff? Is it planned out with an agenda? Do the activities and learning align with your school-wide goals? Without a doubt, leaders who possess Administrator Clarity and reserve this time with staff for professional learning opportunities, team collaboration, data analysis, and action planning see an increase in focus and thus in results.

Are you wondering what those staff meetings actually look like? Let's take a deep dive into one of Sandy's meeting agendas with the Dynamic Learning Academy (see Table 5.3 on page 44). As you can see, she included her sixty-second update. This was a strategy Sandy often used to let her staff know about upcoming due dates, districtwide reminders, or other operational information that was important but did not require discussion. This allowed her to get that information to everyone and then focus the rest of the meeting on instruction.

On this particular day, the school was focusing on the recent benchmark assessment data and analyzing that data to determine the next steps for Tier I intervention and possible Tier II interventions. At this point, the school was relatively new to learning cycles and had created annual grade-level SMART goals for only two years before the pandemic. The staff had never been through the entire learning cycle process from beginning to end. This was going to be their first experience with analyzing grade-level data and then creating a short-term SMART goal for their Tier I instruction as well as their first time truly identifying students who might need Tier II support with prerequisite skills based on current data.

Sandy took time during this meeting to model the process she expected her teachers to use. She moved through the data analysis protocol that they would be using during their collaboration time the following day, and she also modeled how to generate an appropriate SMART goal based on the analysis of the data.

Once this process was completed, Sandy checked for understanding and then provided clarity about her expectations for the product. The teams had the remaining time during the meeting to start this activity, which they would complete by the end of the week. Sandy provided clarity about the outcome of this meeting (a short-term SMART goal for each grade level based on data analysis from the most recent assessment), and she ensured that her staff had a shared understanding of what the expectations were for this process.

Dynamic Learning Academy

Dynamic Learning Academy is dedicated to educating confident, lifelong learners by providing academic rigor, ensuring a dynamic and inclusive learning environment, and providing flexible and innovative learning.

Date: April 7, 2021   Time: 3:00–4:00

Agenda Items	Notes	Time
Be Present, Be Engaged, Be Open		
Positive postcards	• Write at least two positive postcards to students. Turn them in to the office, and we will send them out.	5 min.
Sixty-second update for the week	• Kids and Health Office • CAASPP Testing Schedule • PTA Bookfair • Sign up for monthly Counselor Classroom Visit » Topic: College and Careers	1 min.
Focus on learning	• PLC Question 3: How will we respond when some students do not learn? • Benchmark Data Analysis Protocol • SMART Goal development • Target students for Tier II • Next steps for your PLC	50 min.
Closing	• Questions • RAFFLE!	4 min.

Table 5.3. Sample Staff Meeting Agenda

Step 5: Stay the Course

Without question, we all will experience a time when an operational task needs to be addressed and may even derail our perfectly planned staff meeting on common formative assessments or intervention team planning.

As school leaders, our role has always been defined by our ability to keep student and staff learning at the forefront. In a typical year, we expect the variety of challenges and curveballs to temporarily distract us from our purpose. As an intentional leader, you need to fight the urge and stay the course.

We understand the challenges brought on since the pandemic began in March 2020. At times, you may feel that there is an omnipresent magnetic force field pulling your attention away from learning and redirecting your focus to health and safety protocols, personal protective equipment, measuring tape, arrival and dismissal procedures, and classroom setup. These items are extremely important and necessary, but they are not always at the core of your passion and purpose. We understand that you are going to feel conflicted knowing that you will have to sacrifice plans for growth and learn to make room for the implementation of health and safety.

In these moments, we ask you to turn to one of the most intentional leaders we know, John Wooden, for insight and encouragement during difficult times:

> "Stay the course. When thwarted, try again; harder; smarter. Persevere relentlessly." —John Wooden

If ever there was a time in education when you need to persevere relentlessly, it is now! Despite the magnetic distractions, following your plan with the goal in mind can help you stay the course. Yes, there will be days, no doubt, when that pull will feel strong. Those are the days when you need to rely on your friends, your colleagues, and your mentors to bring you back.

We are in a time when we can no longer use COVID as an excuse not to try again and again, harder and smarter. Be relentless in the learning of both your staff and your students until the very end. And when you feel that magnetic force pulling you away from your goals, reach out to a friend, text a colleague, find that person who grounds you in your "why." Let them bring you back, and then, stay the course.

Here are three tips we recommend to help you stay the course:

1. *Plan, plan, plan.* Create a learning plan for staff and students. Ask yourself where your school should place its focus during a set time (e.g., the whole year, the weeks between Thanksgiving and Winter Break, the last month of school). Assessments? Interventions? SMART goals? Make a plan to ensure that one of these goals happens. Set dates. Backward map from your goal.

2. *Articulate the goal.* Publicly share the goal with students, staff, and the community. Research shows that the more one publicly shares specific goal-oriented plans, the more likely one is to achieve them.

3. *Iterate.* Monitor your goal and iterate as needed. Don't believe that changing your path to your goal is failure—it is just another way to get to your destination.

Step 6: Monitor the Progress, Not Just the Outcome

Just as teachers consistently monitor their students' progress toward learning targets, as administrators we need to monitor our teachers' progress toward the school-wide goal. Do they have the structures and skills to meet that goal? Do we need to intervene and provide some targeted support to keep them on track?

Here are some quick tips to help you focus on this *process* as a means to support your teachers in finishing this school year strong.

Check In

As a leader, put agreed-upon assessment dates that grade-level teams have committed to on *your* calendar. As principals, when teacher teams identified when they were going to administer a common formative assessment on comprehension of informative text, we would add that date to our calendars so that we knew when to follow up with the team. We would intentionally ask them about their data and how their students were progressing. This was one of the key areas our schools had focused on, so we made it a priority to know what was happening within the classrooms, not just at meetings. Teachers shared with us how much they appreciated the involvement and the fact that we made this a priority for the students, the teachers, and our administrative team as well. Following up with your grade levels before and after their assessments is an easy strategy to get a pulse for what learning is happening throughout the year.

Be sure when you check in that you are focused on the learning. Ask team members about their goals and about the growth toward the goals. What do they need from you to support their students in achieving these short-term goals?

Step 7: Celebrate Success

In Chapter 11, we elaborate on celebration and recognition in greater depth, but here we want to highlight the importance of this step in the implementation process. Celebration of the process is critical in motivating all those involved and letting them know that they are on the right path. Teaching and learning are arduous and exhausting. School leadership should be highlighting the celebrations and the path forward. Efforts on the part of students and staff should be genuinely recognized, and celebrations of student learning and success should be ongoing throughout the entire school year. This is the fuel that helps you stay the course and achieve your goal.

Chapter Highlights

- Start with the end in mind.
- Develop a clear plan for articulating the goals to everyone, implement your plan, stay the course, and celebrate successes.
- Your goals should drive your yearlong planning and actions. Every staff meeting, collaborative planning time, and extended day time should be intentionally planned out to align with the goals.

Chapter 6

RESOURCE ALLOCATION

Intentional leaders with clarity understand that values are communicated on the basis of where we allocate our time and our money. As an intentional school leader, you use transparent budgeting aligned with school goals to allocate time and money to the highest priorities. This chapter provides anecdotes and resources for school leaders looking to intentionally align their budgets with goals.

The idea of transparent budgeting and resource allocation can seem scary and overwhelming. If you are anything like us, you may not have had formal instruction on this concept. Ours consisted of perhaps one budget overview class in our administrative credential program. We are here to break down the concept of transparent budgeting to provide clarity for both you as a school leader and your key stakeholders so you can appropriately and effectively allocate funds that positively impact student learning.

I've Got My Plan—How Do I Implement It?

You developed goals, you created a plan, and now you need to ensure that your plan happens. Each year, most school leaders are tasked with implementing the annual plan that supports the school-wide goals. Often, our plans require professional learning opportunities, additional staff, and supplemental programs tied to a variety of funding streams. You may have funding with limited restrictions, or you may be allotted funding that is intended to supplement learning that targets specific students who require additional support, such as English learners, socio-economically disadvantaged students, or students who are experiencing homelessness or are in foster care. Whatever funding you are allocated, it is imperative that money is aligned with goals and spent on evidence-based practices.

Invest in People, Not Programs

Too often, we hear from school leaders who are not sure how best to spend the thousands, even hundreds of thousands, of dollars they are allocated and thus end up spending money on a multitude of programs that we call the "shiny golden tickets." On any given day, our inboxes are inundated with emails from companies and people wanting us to buy their products. Each email provides "research" to indicate that its product will indeed increase student achievement and be the golden ticket to meeting our school goals. Some of these emails even identify specific funding sources we might use to purchase their program.

When thinking about spending money that is aligned with your school goals *and* that will help make the impact you expect to see, it is imperative to focus not just on what works but on what works best given time constraints, and the financial and human capital investment needed for full implementation.

We want to stress the importance of spending money on evidence-based practices. As a quick review, evidence-based practices are those practices and programs that "have evidence to show that they are effective at producing results and improving outcomes when implemented" (ESSA, 2015).

Typically, this evidence is produced from formal research and studies. While there are many online resources that list a plethora of evidence-based practices, we typically turn to John Hattie's meta-analyses of what works best in education and learning. The exhaustive list of his Visible Learning research is always changing on the basis of continued analysis of current studies, and it is a valuable hub that points you in the right direction of where best to place your emphasis and finances to implement your plan. The most up-to-date research on Visible Learning can be found at https://visible-learning.org.

While we know there will be times when certain programs may need to be purchased to help with monitoring student learning and organizing learning data in a way that enables teachers to have immediate access for ease of analysis, we suggest investing in your people. This includes long-range plans that include opportunities to build capacity among your staff, help them develop habits around best practices for student learning, and also honor their time and learning through additional compensation.

When allocating funds to support the implementation of your plan, ask yourself these questions:

- Is the plan sustainable?
- Will it yield both short-term and long-term results?
- Is it manageable given the time constraints and funding sources available?

We will focus on that last question. Any program or plan can work. But what will be required to fully implement that plan to see results?

We all have those boxed programs collecting dust in a room on our campuses. Well, you can imagine that at one point, one of those boxes was the shiny golden ticket for student success for our schools. The program seemed perfect. It was a box of lessons by grade-level span designed for any teacher to implement small-group intervention with minimal planning and ease. The box contained targeted skill-based lessons that were scripted on laminated cards and organized by reading and writing domains. What a perfect way to implement small-group instruction in a focused manner, right?

Once those boxes were purchased, unwrapped, and opened, teachers began to use them in a variety of ways. Some used them as their core instruction for teaching grammar skills, others used them only for students who had scored below proficiency level on the prior year's state assessment, and others used them for students who needed more time and support with a specific concept. We did not have a plan for systematic implementation. We did not have a system for identifying students for our small-group instruction, including how to create pre- and post-assessments to create fluid groups of students who would be the target audiences for this program. We did not have continued professional learning opportunities related to the use of this product, aside from the initial overview of what each box contained. As you can imagine, after a year or two of sporadic use, the boxes made their way into the cupboards of classrooms, never to be used again.

This story is all too common in our schools. We are often drawn to the shiny golden ticket because it seems easier, when in reality there are foundational systems that must be in place for the program to be effective. We implore you to invest in these systems by investing in your people and their learning; build habits around best practices, and provide times for authentic collaboration. Ensure continued learning opportunities for new strategies and programs that support both new and veteran users of the programs and strategies. Commit to focusing on the implementation rather than the results.

We encourage you to remember that you are a steward of public funds. Those funds are not infinite, and your decisions about how to use them can have a direct impact on student achievement. *If* you decide to allocate funds to programs, make sure you couple that with intensive and systematic implementation and funding to support long-term implementation and progress.

One School's Example

When Sandy and Carin were an administration team together, the school's needs assessment indicated that our English learners were not meeting either their language proficiency goals or their academic goals in reading. We were not reclassifying our English learners at the expected rate, and in fact our total school achievement on the state testing was significantly lower than the average scores of similar schools in our district. Being new to the site, we had not yet developed relationships with our staff and did not know what practices and instructional habits were already in place. After meeting with our leadership team to review the results of the needs assessment and discuss some options for our school-wide goals that year, we decided to leverage by committing to implementing an evidence-based strategy called structured student discourse.

Through structured student talk routines embedded throughout all content areas, all students, especially our English learners, would have multiple opportunities to process and express their learning of new content in a way that supported their use of academic vocabulary and helped them transition this communication to their writing. After meeting with leadership teams, staff, and our parent community, we thought this seemed like an effective focus area that would be relatively easy to implement in the short term but would have long-lasting effects on student learning. The scalability seemed plausible, the cost to implement was minimal, and we could use teacher leaders to help with implementation in the classroom.

Planning and Funding

We had the goal and we had the plan. The next step was allocating funding to support implementation of the plan. With our limited funding sources, we decided to invest most of the money in the professional learning of staff over the course of the school year and reserve a small percentage for supplemental resources to help teachers implement the structured talk routines. We used a chart similar to Table 6.1 to help us map out our plan and align it directly with our funding.

Site Goal #1

Action Steps	Funding Source and Amount	Evidence	Resources	Time Line
What action steps will we take to make progress toward our goal?	What funding will be needed to support the actions?	What evidence will we use to measure progress?	What are the best resources?	What is an appropriate time line for the action steps?

Site Goal #2

Action Steps	Funding Source and Amount	Evidence	Resources	Time Line
What action steps will we take to make progress toward our goal?	What funding will be needed to support the actions?	What evidence will we use to measure progress?	What are the best resources?	What is an appropriate time line for the action steps?

Table 6.1. Long-Range Plan Aligned with Funding Sources

In summary, while every aspect of Administrator Clarity is important, resource allocation truly defines you as a leader. It is important to remember that *people determine our priorities as school leaders on the basis of where we place our time and our money.*

For this reason, it is critical that our "why" and our goals are directly aligned with our school budget. Any stakeholder should be able to pick up our school budget and immediately know what our school's goals are and how we are making progress toward those goals.

Chapter Highlights

- When thinking about spending money that is aligned with our school's goals *and* will help make the impact we expect to see, it is imperative to focus not just on what works but on what works best given time constraints and the financial and human capital investment needed for full implementation.

- People determine our priorities as school leaders on the basis of where we place our time and our money.

SECTION 3

Clarity of Communication

Chapter 7

YOU KNOW YOUR "WHY," BUT HAVE YOU COMMUNICATED IT?

One of the biggest mistakes made by new and veteran administrators is in their communication style and choices. This chapter dives into concepts such as communicating with authenticity and purpose and infusing stories into your communication.

Failing Forward—a Leadership Example to Ponder

Sometimes we think, as school leaders, that we have been crystal clear in our message, only to hear the message come back to us as if delivered via some distorted game of "telephone." Take this example.

> Principal Alvarez determined that it was important to share with her school the need for teachers to review the most recent benchmark assessment data from their quarterly math assessment. She decided to bring together her leadership team to discuss this matter. She clearly knew that her school-wide goal was to decrease the opportunity gap for some of her marginalized student groups, specifically in math. While school data showed overall gains, the aforementioned student groups did not experience gains commensurate with the rest

of the student body. She brought her leadership team into her conference room and shared the following:

"Team, I've been reviewing our benchmark assessment data in math. I want to start by sharing how happy I am with the overall progress that we have made. Our school's student improvement score is 7 percent above the district average and 11 percent above our goal. At this point, I'd like you to go back to your grade-level teams and take a deep dive into the data. What can we do better? What are our next steps? We will come back together in two weeks and share with each other what our teams have come up with."

Imagine Ms. Alvarez's surprise when one of her teachers came to her the following week and shared this information:

"Ms. Alvarez, I wanted to give you a heads-up. The staff is pretty upset. They have been working really hard in the area of math. They have exceeded both your goals and the district goals. They feel like they will never be good enough. Even with all of their accomplishments, you are asking them to go back into their data and decide what they can do better. There are rumblings among the staff that they want to transfer. They never feel that they are good enough for you."

Ms. Alvarez thanked the teacher for her time, closed the door to her office, phoned her mentor principal friend, and left this message:

"Hi, Joan, it's me. I need your feedback. It feels like no matter what I do here, I'm the bad guy. I just don't know what I am doing wrong. Maybe I'm not cut out for this job. Call me back. Thanks."

This brief anecdote illustrates how a lack of Administrator Clarity in any one small area can lead to frustration for both the teaching staff and the school leader. It can in turn increase feelings of frustration and hostility on both sides. While Ms. Alvarez clearly knew where she wanted to go and what she wanted teachers to uncover, her *lack of clarity* left staff feeling that they were not good enough. Rather than be specific about her purpose and her intention in this communication, she left it open-ended. She was positive and celebratory with her small group, but by the time her message made its way around the campus, that was not the overall teacher impression.

Any school leader who has led a school of more than five teachers has lived some version of this example. It is normal and at times feels unavoidable.

So, what could Ms. Alvarez have done differently? This anecdote, on its face, makes it seem as if Ms. Alvarez did everything perfectly. She brought in her leadership team. She shared a celebration with her team for having met goals, and then she empowered team members to go back and create a plan for the next steps. Why did this communication exchange result in rumblings of teachers transferring?

Ms. Alvarez's main mistake was directly rooted in the lack of clarity in her communication. Although she clearly knew the school-wide goal was to decrease the opportunity gap for some of her marginalized student groups, specifically in math, she had not communicated this school-wide goal to her team. She looked at the school data and realized that it showed overall gains, yet the student groups who she believed should have been targeted did not experience gains commensurate with the rest of the student body.

In contrast, her teachers looked at this data and thought they had met and exceeded district goals for the school. When Ms. Alvarez sent them back to analyze their data, they could not help but feel defeated and frustrated. Ms. Alvarez struggled to communicate with clarity. This is the first type of communication we will discuss because it is a critical step in fostering a responsive school culture.

Communicating with Clarity

Often, as school leaders we believe that we have communicated with clarity only to find out later that we missed the mark. It is not surprising that because we live, eat, and breathe our school's goals and we are certain we have mentioned them a few times in our staff meetings, we expect that our teachers will know these goals, internalize them as we do, and be able to receive our intended message.

We spent significant time early in this book discussing the importance of developing our "why," but it is equally critical that we also clearly communicate our "why" in all that we say and do.

Just as we, as school leaders, seem to have a thousand things flying at us at any given moment, so do our teachers. Our communication to our staff needs to be intentional, repetitive, multimodal, and rooted in our purpose. We need to keep our words sparse at times so that they have an impact. It is important that our purpose and our "why" are anchored in all that we do and all that we say to our staff.

We have found that communicating our reasoning has helped our staff to better understand our purpose and to support our direction. Below are some sample sentence frames to assist you in driving decisions and conversations back to your "why" as a school.

Situation: In a staff meeting (setting purpose)

General Example: The objective of today's meeting is _____ , and this is important because it ties into our school-wide goal of _____ . As you know, our "why" for this goal is _____ . And we feel that _____ will help us get there by _____ .

Specific Example: The objective of today's staff meeting is to examine recent ELA subgroup assessment data. It will get us closer to closing the gap for our students with disabilities. As you know, our "why" for this goal is that we have a current discrepancy of 50% in proficiency between the achievement of our general education population and the achievement of our special education population, and we recognize that it is our professional and ethical obligation to close this gap because we believe all students are capable of learning. We believe that by examining this data, we can craft a plan, with your input, to begin to take the steps necessary to get closer to our goal and keep us rooted in our "why."

Situation: When a teacher makes a request in line with the school's "why"

General Example: Thank you for taking the time today to come and present your idea with me. I am so excited at how well this aligns with our "why" of _____ . I appreciate that as a staff member, you continue to come up with ideas and lessons aligned with what we believe as a staff, and I look forward to supporting you on this journey.

Specific Example: Thank you for taking the time today to come and present your idea with me. I am so excited at how well this aligns with our "why" of closing the achievement gap for our students with disabilities. I appreciate that as a staff member, you continue to come up with ideas and lessons aligned with what we believe as a staff, and I look forward to supporting you in this journey.

Situation: When a teacher makes a request not in line with the school's "why"

General Example: Thank you for taking the time today to come and present your idea with me. My initial reaction is that this doesn't align well with our "why" of _____ . However, I'd like some time to think more about how we can work with your ideas and align them with our "why." Can you also see if there is a way that you can more closely align this initiative with our "why," and we can reconvene early next week to dive deeper into these ideas?

Specific Example: Thank you for taking the time today to come to me and present your idea on changing common planning time. My initial reaction is that this doesn't align closely with our "why" of supporting the achievement of our students with disabilities and closing the achievement gap. I worry that not having common planning time will not allow for teachers to come together and discuss the strategies that work best for them in closing these gaps. However, I'd like some time to think more about how we can work with your ideas and align them with our "why." Can you also see if there is a way that you can more closely align this initiative with our "why," and we can reconvene early next week to dive deeper into these ideas?

Early in our careers in school leadership, we believed it was enough to have strategic goals, progress monitoring benchmarks, and a clearly articulated pathway to meet those goals. And yet it did not take long for us to realize that we never inspired anyone by having goals. Don't get us wrong—strategic planning is *critical* in school leadership. Over time, we began to realize that strategic planning and goal creation are most effective when coupled with compelling justification and relentless passion for why these goals are needed. We realized that it was not enough to say, "In the school year 2021–2022, students in the bottom quartile will increase their math proficiency by 15 percent as measured by state assessments."

The truth is, while it is appropriate for a school-wide plan to include such goals, the plan itself does not inspire action or passion. Even though it may tell our teachers clearly what we should strive to do, it does not make them believe in the importance of the cause.

When we, as leaders with Administrator Clarity, begin goal setting and strategic planning, we practice backward mapping. We begin by determining *why* we need to do what we need to do. When we can communicate this to our stakeholders, our *what* (goals and benchmarks) plays in the background to why we are doing it.

At times, goals can feel lofty and even unattainable in the face of all that educational professionals must balance each and every day. It is easy to dismiss goals as too challenging or too difficult.

We contend that the very best leaders spend much time, energy, and passion creating a compelling "why" for their "what." Then even the most unattainable of goals seems both within reach and absolutely necessary. Teams become inspired, and educators achieve far beyond what they ever dreamed possible because they collectively believe in the mission.

> *A well-thought-out and compelling "why" that is squarely focused on providing the very best opportunities of educational equity for all students can rarely be dismissed.*

We assert that in conversations with your staff, more than 50 percent of your time should be spent discussing your "why." The "what" and "how" matter, but your staff will not hear them or see them as important if you do not have their hearts.

School leaders with Administrator Clarity share their "why" as they focus on each decision they make on their campus and in every discussion they have with staff and families.

School leaders who are intentional are constantly thinking about why they are managing every decision in a certain way, and they iterate and change their approach when presented with new information.

In the anecdote presented earlier, Ms. Alvarez did *a lot* right. She celebrated teacher success; she brought in a group of stakeholders; she elicited teacher feedback in making future goals. Her communication failure and lack of clarity came before this communication exchange ever happened. Ms. Alvarez was focused on performance for a specific group of students who were not making growth commensurate with the rest of the student body, but she did not communicate this with her staff.

What if, instead of a leadership meeting pushing teachers to go back and find the problem, Ms. Alvarez had owned her part in this shortcoming and elicited help from her teachers by recognizing their strengths and restating her "why," which was missing from previous communications?

What if Ms. Alvarez had instead led the meeting as follows with her full staff?

> "Staff, I have been reviewing our data. We are knocking it out of the park with our assessment scores, and as a result of your hard work, we have not only met but exceeded school, district, and state benchmarks in math. This was a job well done. Take a moment to share with your table partner one way that you contributed to our school's success.
>
> "Now, I want to share with you that I am incredibly happy and filled with joy based on all you have accomplished—*and* there is more work to be done.
>
> "What I failed to share when we met at this time last year was that despite our tremendous forward momentum in math, we have some disparities as a school that we need to dive into.

What I failed to share last year is that we have not met the needs of all of our students. We currently have a small group of students from traditionally marginalized backgrounds who are not demonstrating the same academic performance and growth as their peers of the same age and grade. I knew this last year, and I created this as a goal in my mind as an area for us to improve. I failed to share this with you. As I review our new data this year, while I can celebrate the growth we have made overall, I realize that I have a moral and ethical obligation to share with each of you my 'why' for this school year.

"This year, every decision I make, and every dollar I spend, will be rooted in remedying this opportunity gap for our marginalized students. While I want *every* student in our school to succeed, I also want to dive deeply into why we are having success overall—as a school—yet are not making those same gains with these groups and intervening as necessary.

"I also want to share that I need help with this. This is not something I can do alone. You have all shown me that you can increase achievement. You are go-getters who meet goals. Now I need us to come together and examine the data I shared regarding our marginalized groups, and I need your help in developing a plan to shine our greatness onto another group of amazing students."

In this communication, Ms. Alvarez did a few things differently, which will make all the difference to her staff. First, she was clear that this year, her "why" or purpose was to close the gap for marginalized students. She also owned that some of the inability to meet her goal was that she had not articulated this goal with them. She owned her shared responsibility. She also expressed a request for assistance. Rather than make the presumption, as many administrators do, that "I pay you, you meet my goals," she requested a partnership in meeting these goals and acknowledged the skills and strengths each member of her team brings to the table.

While communication with teachers can be nuanced, multifaceted, and even flawed at times, if you lead every conversation anchored in your "why" and clearly center your goals and beliefs on it, teachers will begin to listen, and, more important, they will begin to hear what you say.

Leaders cannot have Administrator Clarity if their staff do not know what the leader stands for, what the goals are, and what the plan is to get there.

Chapter Highlights

- In conversations with your staff, more than 50 percent of your time should be spent discussing your "why." While the "what" and "how" matter, those will not be heard or seen as important if you do not have their hearts.

- Anchor every conversation in your "why," and clearly center your goals and beliefs on it. When you do so, teachers will begin to listen, and, more important, they will begin to hear what you say.

Chapter 8

COMMUNICATING WITH AUTHENTICITY AND VULNERABILITY

When you become a school administrator, everyone has advice for you on *how* you should lead. The reality is that no one can really tell you how to lead and communicate because the moment you take this advice and try to be something you are not is the moment you experience failure. Success in communication comes at the exact moment that your communication style honors who you are as a leader and comes from your authentic self. This chapter explores the importance of leading a school with authenticity.

The truth is that when a needs assessment is completed with a group of stakeholders to inquire about what type of communication they would like to see in their next leader, they will have a lot of great responses.

They might respond with words like "strong," "dynamic," "charismatic," "diverse," "honest," "compassionate," and "kind." *What often does not emerge is the term "authentic."* There is an assumption that this is an unspoken rule, but the reality is that many leaders stretch to reflect so many of the other qualities that they lose touch with who they are and their authentic self in the process.

People want to be led by someone authentic. This is partly a reaction to the turbulent times we live in. It is also a response to how inauthentic our Facebook/Instagram/Snapchat/LinkedIn, and other social media–driven world appears right now. There is widespread disenchantment with politicians and businesspeople. We all suspect that we are seeing an airbrushed version of reality.

We, as a generation, have become increasingly dissatisfied with fake and "perfect" leaders and their polished LinkedIn profiles. Going viral as we write this book is the LinkedIn profile of a woman who removed her glossy headshot and replaced it with a real and candid photo.

Just as it has in our world, authenticity has become an increasingly desirable quality in today's schools. It is a quality that, unfortunately, is in short supply. Principals and teachers both associate authenticity with sincerity, honesty, and integrity. When staff see these qualities, they realize that they are the attributes that uniquely define great leaders.

School leaders often assume that authenticity is something someone is born with—a leader is either authentic or not. The paradoxical challenge for a school leader is that you cannot tell someone you are authentic. People must develop this opinion on their own. You do not have control over whether or not they believe this. In truth, it is difficult for leaders to find a balance between expressing their personalities and managing those of the people they aspire to lead or at least influence.

The importance of authenticity cannot be overstated. A school leader who can be both transparent, visionary, and true to their authentic self is a challenge that can often distinguish leaders who make an impact.

Authentic school leaders remain focused on where they are going but never lose sight of where they came from. Highly attuned to their environments, they continue to keep in mind their audience, their purpose, and the intention of their communication interaction. They retain their distinctiveness as individuals, yet they know how to win acceptance in strong district mandates and social cultures, and know how to use elements of those cultures as a basis for radical change.

We believe that authentic and humble principals are more likely to create healthier and more effective school cultures, develop staff potential, boost team morale, and increase overall school and student academic achievement.

Failing Forward—a Leadership Example to Ponder

In the examples below we compare two new school leaders. Both are in similar situations yet one has the courage to be authentic and vulnerable while the other struggles to maintain her image. The outcomes may surprise you.

Ms. Demetrius was meeting her new staff for the very first time. It was her opening staff meeting with a group of one hundred teachers and staff members. Their county, for the first time in a long while, had not selected a leader from within the district. None of the staff had been on the interview team, and none of them knew what to expect.

As their new school leader, she knew, above all else, that this was her only chance to make a first impression, and whatever she led with would be their first impression of her. She spent a lot of time and thought long and hard about every piece of advice she had ever been given. Then she thought about how her new boss, the superintendent, would be there, watching her as she approached her new staff and introduced herself. She knew that she would never get a second chance to make a first impression.

She spent hours and labored away at the most exquisite overview of all of her accomplishments. She shared details about every award she had won and every recognition received.

Next, she reviewed the data from the school she was entering. She analyzed what they were doing well and where they were falling short. She developed a list of five goals, based solely on data, and created action steps for implementation. There is no doubt that this presentation was spot-on and top-notch.

The day finally came for her to be introduced to her new staff. The superintendent came to the front of the auditorium, completed a short welcome and introduction, and left her to begin forming connections with her new staff.

Slightly disturbed that the amazing presentation she had prepared specifically for his eyes would remain unseen by him, she moved forward in her presentation. Sadly, her new staff had been through their share of school leaders. They knew this drill all too well. They listened attentively at first, seeking points of connection. But what they heard from her was all too close to what they had heard from the four others who had preceded her in the past seven years. They began to get fidgety by the time she got to the third slide of her accomplishments and justifications as to why she was fit to lead them. Several began to whisper, and then the group text chat began.

Sensing she was losing her audience, she regained her poise, read the room, and quickly moved into her data-developed goals for the school. But it was too late to turn back; the text chat had already begun.

"Oh look, she says we need to work on the ELA scores of our students with disabilities. Guess I will tell that to the three teachers who quit last year over the union debacle."

And then, "Yes, I just love it when people come in and tell us how to do our jobs when they don't even know us."

And so it went for another twenty-five minutes.

Ms. Demetrius ended by sharing how excited she was to be a part of their amazing school, gave them some compliments, and let them know she would stay afterward for anyone who wanted to come up and speak with her. Then she dismissed them. Staff members rushed out of the auditorium like students before a three-day weekend, and she stood there as one remaining teacher walked up to her. The following exchange happened.

"Hi, I'm Maritza. I teach Spanish classes here, and I want to welcome you to our school. We've been through a lot these past four years, so don't mind them too much; they will come around. It's a tough staff. I really hope you can win them over. I wish you well."

Ms. Demetrius thanked Maritza and invited her to come to her office sometime and share more details with her, and off Maritza went.

Ms. Demetrius stood there for a moment, in a combination that could only be described as disappointment and shock. Her masterfully crafted presentation was not seen by her new supervisor, and perhaps her impact on her staff was less than what she had hoped for. She was confused. She had followed nearly every piece of advice she had ever received about coming in new to a school. She had incorporated everything she had read in her school leadership books. She was left dejected, knowing she still had a mountain to climb.

Ms. Demetrius *had* followed every piece of advice she had read in her leadership books. She had carefully analyzed the data and studied the school. Her presentation was nearly flawless, so why did it fall on deaf ears?

The staff at that school had been through this song and dance before. They had seen principal after principal come into their school. They had watched these principals share their previous accomplishments, create goals, and develop action steps. They had watched as their principals sat at the helm of their schools, unaware of and even sometimes unconcerned with what was happening within the school walls.

They had worked with principals who had these exact same credentials and plans, and they had been disappointed by them, again and again. While Ms. Demetrius was different and would prove that to them over time, she now had the additional task of overcoming a lukewarm first impression.

Let's compare her opening staff meeting with that of one of her best friends, Ms. Thomas.

It was Ms. Thomas's opening staff meeting with a group of one hundred teachers and staff whom she had never met. Their county, for the first time in a long while, had not selected a leader from within the district. None of the staff members had been on the interview team, and none of them knew what to expect.

As their new school leader, she knew, above all else, that this was her only chance to make a first impression, and whatever she led with would be their first impression of her.

And then she took every single piece of leadership advice that had ever been given to her and threw it out the window.

She had been coached about how to handle this moment by her first principal, who mentored her in leadership. He taught her to be strong. He urged her to have strong convictions, to never let them see her sweat, and above all else to present herself as confident, unwavering, and infallible. As he reasoned, people needed to know their leaders could lead.

And—she did not follow his advice. She did not tell her audience about all the great things she had planned for their school. She did not share a laundry list of accomplishments to put them at ease so they would know she was qualified for the job. She did not even tell them that she was well-intentioned, thoughtful, and reflective. She did not spend one minute of that first two hours discussing a single piece of data or a single school goal.

Instead, she opened with the story of one of the biggest mistakes she had made as a school leader. It went against nearly all traditional logic. And because this was so much unlike any opening from any other principal in a meeting like this, the superintendent did not leave, as he ordinarily would. He pulled up a seat and sat down to listen.

She told them what she fondly called the "Quilt Story." As the story went, it was her first year as a principal and she was well-intentioned, idealistic, and eager. She loved and valued her staff and wanted nothing more than to make them feel appreciated. She decided to spend the summer renovating their staff lounge and creating a space that would make them feel comfortable and special. Hanging on the wall of the lounge was a large quilt. Scanning the names, she soon realized this quilt had names of people who had not been at the school for over ten years. She reasoned that it no longer represented current staff and carefully removed the quilt to replace it with an *amazing* recognition wall.

Ms. Thomas recounted the Quilt Story to her new staff, describing the amazing new space and throwing in great flowery language. Then she told them why that had been an epic failure. It had come back to her, a year or two later, that for a variety of reasons this decision, while well-intentioned, had been hurtful and had not delivered the message in her heart.

So, Ms. Thomas essentially opened her first meeting with a brand-new staff by sharing with them one way she had failed as a leader. Her decision to start there was *intentional* and *strategic*. She caught her superintendent's attention as someone who thought outside the box and led with authenticity. She caught her staff's attention as someone who might just be a little different from all the others.

Here were her two "whys" behind her message.

First, she was an outsider to her new school and district. Her new staff's biggest fear was that even if she was a nice person (which she was), she would mess up their flow. Maybe she would be quick to react and their school would suffer as a result. What a wonderful way for her to tell them she had already made that mistake and learned her lesson. They got to hear that she would come in and honor their customs and she would watch and learn. She could have just said that, but in illustrating that via a story, she created context and credibility. She was intentional in her humility and vulnerable in that she was not the expert of their school.

Second, she wanted them to be brave. She wanted to let them know she was not a perfect leader. She knew she would not make that mistake again, but it was pretty much a foregone conclusion that she would make others. She surmised that if she were willing to fail, perhaps they would be more willing to as well. She was intentional in her authenticity and vulnerability, and she made it clear they should not expect perfection, and neither did she.

She ended by sharing how excited she was to be a part of their amazing school, gave them some compliments, and let them know she would stay afterward for anyone who wanted to come up and speak with her. Then she dismissed them.

Something strange happened that struck the superintendent as different from the way these meetings usually went. Staff members did not rush out of the auditorium; instead, they lingered. They walked up to her, either individually or within their professional learning community (PLC) groups. They welcomed her. They said they were excited to get to know her. They made appointments to pop into her office. A couple of them even shared funny fails from their last "pandemic school year." After about an hour of this small talk, the superintendent walked Ms. Thomas out to her car. He looked her squarely in the eyes and said, "You are exactly who this school needs right now."

What is interesting about these two stories is that Ms. Demetrius and Ms. Thomas are best friends. Their leadership style makes them almost clones of each other. Their schools and staff are also very similar and have very similar cultures, climates, and experiences. To be fair, Ms. Demetrius and Ms. Thomas are both exactly what their schools need right now. They both will excel and lead their schools to fabulous success.

When their meetings are done, they will share their opening staff meeting experiences with each other. Ms. Demetrius will pull some pages from Ms. Thomas's book on authenticity, which will help her move forward as she tries to connect with her staff.

Often when people think of Administrator Clarity, there is a huge emphasis on the transactional components of the job. Clearly articulating goals and engaging in open, frequent communication are on all school leaders' to-do lists. What often sets apart a good administrator from a great one is the human connection. Sometimes being responsible for hundreds of staff members and thousands of students can be emotionally draining, and compassion overload can set in. Principals forget that their teachers are human, and at times they forget that they too are human. When you are held up as the example and model, it is difficult to have the bravery to be real.

Leadership itself and what a good leader "should do" have drastically changed over the past few decades. Dave McKeown aptly expressed this in his *Inc.* article "9 Alternative Ways to Lead with Authenticity": "Our concept of leadership continually evolves as we as a species evolve. Just think about some of the Industrial Age practices that emerged from the early studies of leadership. ... The principles applied then are unrecognizable to the current philosophies around meaning, mindfulness, and authenticity. You never stop evolving as a leader. You constantly need to tweak, change and sometimes abandon your methods" (McKeown 2019).

Suggestions for Increasing Authenticity

By utilizing some suggestions made by Dave McKeown in his article "9 Alternative Ways to Lead with Authenticity" and combining these with our own personal insights, we have created a set of 10 steps to help leaders increase their authenticity:

1. Share your purpose, not your goals.

2. Teach them how to make good decisions, then leave it to them.

3. Be a coach, not a boss.

4. Get evaluated by your peers.

5. Have your team tell stories AND tell stories yourself.

6. Ask your team what they feel, not what they think.

7. Care, truly care.

8. Manage the perception.

9. Know yourself and others.

10. Use where you come from.

What follows is a practical guide to applying these points to school leadership.

Share Your Purpose, Not Your Goals

This was best explained in the story in Chapter 7 of Ms. Alvarez and her communication to her staff. When people know why you do what you do every day and why that matters to you, they are more inclined to help you achieve these goals. According to John Hattie and his research on collective teacher efficacy, the single most influential factor in student achievement is collective teacher efficacy, with an effect size of 1.57 (Hattie 2012). A school can never achieve this goal without all teachers and administrators on the same page about what matters to their school and why it matters.

Teach Them How to Make Good Decisions, Then Leave It to Them

One common mistake made by rookie and seasoned administrators alike is to micromanage a great staff into being mediocre. When you lead from a perspective that you and only you know best, staff will quickly pull away from shared decision-making and make up their minds on their own. They will hold on to their great ideas and not speak up in ways that will help the school grow and move forward.

Authentic school leaders begin by honoring the idea that they cannot know everything, nor can they be the expert in all areas. If you have shared your "why" in an authentic manner and emphasized its importance in a way that has inspired your staff, they will feel inspired to make decisions that are directly in line with the ones you would make or are at least based on the direction of your goals.

Be a Coach, Not a Boss

We used to joke with our staff that they could call us anything they wanted, but please don't call us the "b" word, "boss." We have always felt that hierarchy overall feels somewhat out of place in education. We are all on the same team, working toward a common goal, and clearly, there are others who are far more expert in their area than we will ever be.

Inauthentic school leaders mistakenly believe that their shiny framed master's degree in educational leadership has miraculously endowed them with the ability to be all things to all people and to tell each of them how to do their job.

When a school leader comes to the position with more of a coaching role, the perspective shifts.

Get Evaluated by Your Peers

By far the scariest and the most useful day in your career as a school leader is the day you seek authentic feedback. While we leaders can have an overall idea of what is and is not going well in school, we also have blind spots. Some of our blind spots are our own coping skills, knowing that we cannot perfect every part of our leadership, every day.

With that said, valuable feedback can be obtained when you exhibit the bravery to ask where you are falling short. These periodic informal surveys of both those who report to you and those at your level will continue to help you grow *if* and only if you are authentic and open enough to honestly review the feedback you receive and be open to sharing this with others and working on your areas of growth. Authentic leaders never stop growing.

Have Your Team Tell Stories (and Tell Stories Yourself)

As school leaders, we live in a data-rich world. We have so much data and information at our fingertips. Data makes leading easy.

Data also makes leading hard. So many school leaders hide behind the data or use data alone to justify benchmarks and goals. No teacher was ever inspired by data. While data may justify our "why," it should never dictate it. Our purpose must always be authentic and aligned with our mission and vision. While the data can assist us in knowing where to focus, leaders who have high levels of Administrator Clarity have learned the value of an authentic narrative.

For those looking to move into school leadership, going to those interviews and dreaming of landing that perfect job, we share a lesson we learned the hard way. After a handful of failed assistant principal interviews, we remember feeling we would never land our dream jobs. We clearly remember meeting one of our administrative mentors for lunch. She looked us in the eyes and gave us the best advice about authentic communication and storytelling that we have ever received in our leadership careers. She told us that our responses to the interview questions were appropriate, yet we failed to tell our story about who we were as leaders. We were inauthentic.

After recovering from the initial blow, we found clarity in our next steps as leaders. We learned the importance of storytelling.

Our mentor reminded us that those people who sat on our interview panels and all the teachers who followed us are human. Like all humans, they make sense of our world and remember things by way of stories. If we could anchor a best practice in a narrative, people would be more likely to remember. When our data was hooked to a compelling tale, people would trust that our words mattered.

Although data will never inspire people, shared stories of triumph always will. This is perhaps the best lesson we learned for leading people and communicating authentically.

Ask Your Team What They Feel, Not What They Think

As school leaders, often we try to take emotion out of leadership for fear that it will cloud our judgment. We believe that involving feelings will take away from the validity of the data or the importance of our work. When we are inauthentic with our staff and we bottle up our emotions, we set the stage for our staff to believe we value only their ideas, not their feelings. If our staff continue to hide how things make them feel and we try to run a school devoid of emotion, we will come to find that emotions can help steer decisions in a more valuable way when they are treated appropriately.

Care, Truly Care

Amelia Harper shared the following in her 2019 article "Principal: Listening to, Caring for Staff's Needs Key to Success": "No matter how diverse their backgrounds and abilities, teachers, principals and students share one thing in common: they are all human. As such, they all have basic human needs to be heard, understood and accepted. While much of education has become sterilized and digitized in modern society, recognizing the very human emotional needs of teachers and students is the responsibility of a good principal."

Some leaders do a great job of pretending to care, but caring is not something that can be faked. Teachers and staff know when you really care. It is not what you say but the level of authenticity in the communication that shows genuine concern.

Manage the Perception

Establishing your authenticity as a principal is multifaceted. First, you have to ensure that your words are consistent with your deeds; otherwise, your staff will never accept you as authentic. Everyone acknowledges and understands the need for consistency when establishing authenticity, but great school leaders do a lot more than pay lip service to it. They live it every moment of the day. Indeed, it is not an exaggeration to say that great leaders are obsessive about embodying their beliefs.

Often, leaders show this not in grand gestures but in the way they operate day in and day out. It is in those thin-sliced moments, as Malcolm Gladwell would call them—the tiny moments throughout the day that truly define who you are as a leader. It is the leader who stops what they are doing to authentically ask and care about a staff member's child or spouse. It is the leader who picks up a broom in the cafeteria or trash in the hallway or pulls a struggling student in for tutoring. Leaders who are willing to model what they look to see in others are seen as authentic.

But it is not enough just to practice what you preach. To get people to follow you, you also have to get them to relate to you. Authentic school leadership requires finding common ground with your school staff. This means that as the school leader, you will have to present different faces to different audiences, a requirement that many people find hard to square with authenticity. You have to understand your audience and realize that your assistant principal, your school board, and an angry parent all require different parts of you to be present when you speak to them.

Know Yourself and Others

Effective school leaders have a high emotional quotient (EQ) and work explicitly to become self-aware and aware of the emotions of those around them. Great leaders are usually trying to accomplish no more than three or four big goals at a time. They are unwavering about these goals; they do not question them, any more than they question themselves. That is because the goals are usually connected in some way to one of the leader's authentic selves. As a leader, your pursuit of the goals, and the way you communicate them to followers, is intense—which naturally promotes the kind of self-disclosure we are talking about and educates you further about your various selves. A good administrator understands that only school leaders with their feet on the ground and their hands in the work are truly admired and followed by those whom they lead.

Use Where You Come From

By the time candidates are promoted to the principalship, they are likely to have been through the role of lead teacher, school coordinator, registrar, and/or assistant principal. Often they have been out of the classroom for some time. When this is coupled with the rapid rate of change happening annually with the principalship, school leaders cannot establish their authenticity unless they can effectively manage their relationship with their past and leverage this to assist them in moving forward.

Authentic leaders use their personal histories to establish common ground with their staff. As a school leader, tapping into stories from the trenches and your classroom experiences will help you make a connection with your staff. It is also important, if appropriate, to acknowledge the ways in which the classroom has changed and even become more challenging since your teaching years.

Finally, it is critically important to remember that the way we speak about our previous schools and experiences speaks more about us than it does about them.

It is incumbent upon principals also to realize that their staff is looking to them as models for their own actions. Here is an experience from one of the authors about the importance of this modeling.

When the global pandemic hit in 2020, schools were shut down nationwide and teachers worked from their homes. In Sandy's school, administrators continued to report to the school sites to keep things moving along.

After limping through the spring of 2020, schools in Sandy's state were set to reopen and provide instruction simultaneously for both face-to-face students and students who preferred to work from their homes. This is Sandy's story.

> That summer before school started, we all worked hard. We worked harder than we had ever worked, deploying devices, changing our systems and processes, and restructuring how we ran our school day in and day out. As the school leader, I was so focused on getting the school up and running and ready to manage all the changes headed our way, I forgot to model for my staff concepts of self-care and emotional well-being. I worked long hours and spent every waking moment obsessing about my job.
>
> When the school year started up, I looked around at my staff. I realized that they were following my example. They were working insane hours, neglecting their families, and burning the candle at both ends. They had created unreasonable and unsustainable expectations for themselves. As I stood up to my staff, preaching concepts of self-care and one day at a time, I realized that I needed to listen to and follow my own advice. I also realized that my actions had led them to believe that I valued our jobs more than our relationships. I had to work explicitly and openly to share with them the ways I was also working toward my own self-care.

While this is Sandy's story, it could really be any one of our stories. Sometimes we become so tied up and so invested in the "work" of education that it is easy to lose sight of the people. Yet when we lose sight of the people, the relationships, and our leadership role as stewards and caretakers, we begin to lose sight of our own efficacy.

Chapter Highlights

- Leadership demands the expression of an authentic self. You cannot try to lead like someone else. In leadership, there is little more admirable than authenticity. Those in your charge and those whom you serve are looking to you. They want you to be predictable, honest, and true. It feels safe for those we serve to have an idea of who we are and what we stand for. Whether that means our leadership is direct, pointed, and goal-oriented or passionate and vulnerable, when we are our authentic selves, people can honor and recognize that who we say we are matches what we demonstrate as leaders.

- Success in communication comes at the exact moment that your communication style honors who you are as a leader and comes from your authentic self.

- It is easy for us as school leaders to forget these wise words and to forget the advantages of building relationships with our teachers. Yet surveys and research have made it explicitly clear that teachers who feel that their voices are heard and that they are supported in their attempts to take risks in order to reach students tend to produce better results.

Chapter 9

LISTENING TO UNDERSTAND

While much ado is made about the importance of communication, as school leaders we often believe that our words are incredibly valuable in setting the tone for our school. And they are. What we sometimes fail to remember is that the way we listen and the times when we choose not to speak are equally important. This chapter explores the importance of listening as it pertains to leading.

> At our schools, one of our PLC and team meeting norms is that we listen to understand instead of listening to reply. As school leaders, we may be among the very worst at following this norm. We always feel that people are looking to us for the answer, so as they speak, we find ourselves scanning our brains in hopes that when there is a break in the speaking, we will have the answer. We find ourselves constantly going back and trying to improve in this area.

The truth is that listening is arguably one of the most difficult skills in communication, and we are getting worse at it. In his book, *Skilled Interpersonal Communication: Research, Theory and Practice*, Owen Hargie shares his research findings and they are astounding. Hargie finds that we spend 45 percent of our day listening to others, which is more than any other communication activity. As school leaders, we would argue that we spend even more time than that actively engaged in listening, with the expectation of problem-solving.

The challenge is that there is a lag between what we *hear* and what we *understand*. Depending upon the individual, it could be a few seconds to as long as a minute. This is where the trouble starts. As school leaders, during that lag time, we may start to listen to ourselves and not to the other person. As a result, our comprehension plummets. In addition, it is challenging to practice empathy *and* engage in problem-solving at the same time. As we think about how we will address the situation being described to us, we become unable to reflect and understand the needs of the speaker.

As school leaders, we surely suffer from the concept of "confirmation bias" as we are listening to our teachers. This bias is based on the presumption that we *all* unintentionally tend to have "selective hearing." Our brains are programmed to pick out facts or aspects of a conversation that support our preexisting beliefs, values, or perceptions. If this is true, then, as leaders, we have to overcome the ways in which our brain is hardwired in order to engage in successful, empathetic communication and listening. It would be easy to say this is not our fault. The *Harvard Business Review* ("7 Tips for Effective Listening" by Tom D. Lewis and Gerald Graham) cites research that while people are able to process information at a rate of over 600 words per minute, most people speak closer to 175 words per minute. This often results in our mind wandering off topic when we are listening. We have to actively exert sustained mental energy to stay engaged with the speaker while not formulating a reply, becoming distracted by the next task on our agenda, or tuning out because our brain has already made an inference about the speaker's intended message.

The following are a few strategies you can practice in order to better hone the skill of listening to understand.

Poise Yourself as an Active Listener

In this example, Sandy reflects on teaching active listening to her students and reminds us that some of what we need to know, we learned in kindergarten.

> When I taught kindergarten, I had a poster in my classroom of a little boy sitting, engaged in active listening. He had his hands folded, his eyes were focused on the teacher, his items were put

away in his desk, and he was sitting up straight and tall. When the students came to the rug each day, we reviewed what it looked like to be an active listener; then students engaged in the practice of this skill.

The reality is that most school and district leaders probably need some reasonable copy of this poster adorning the walls of their offices, just a hair under those advanced degrees. As school leaders, we are constantly busy and our plates always seem a little too full. It is very hard to be an active listener when you have so many imperative tasks looming over your head.

It is commonplace these days to see a teacher pop into an administrator's office, for the administrator to acknowledge the teacher's presence and invite them in, and just as the teacher begins to speak, the administrator begins to look at their laptop, glance at the emails popping in, or pick up the cell phone as it pings.

As school leaders, we must be intentional about putting everything down and focusing.

When we invite a staff member into our office, we should have steps in place to give them our attention and attend to them. We must have a mental image, similar to the "listening" poster in the kindergarten classroom, of what an attentive principal looks like, and we must invite people in to speak with us only when our actions can match that mental image.

If you are not ready to listen, be honest and up-front. Stop what you are doing. Acknowledge the staff member. Let them know that it is important for them to have your full attention, and that at this time you cannot give them that. Pick a future time on your calendar. Set it up with them and assure them that when they return, they will have your undivided attention.

1. Stop.

2. Acknowledge and thank the staff member.

3. Let the staff member know that what they have to say is important to you.

4. Set a future meeting, and place it on your calendar at that moment with the staff member present.

If you decide that you can have a conversation at that moment, prepare and remind yourself what active listening looks like. As the staff member enters, ask him or her to give you a moment so that you can fully prepare to listen to them. Actively close your laptop. Adjust your posture, or move your chair away from the desk and sit squarely facing your staff member. Breathe slowly and deeply. Physically relax and get comfortable. Ask the speaker if they think it would be important for you to take notes, and then sit ... and listen.

Begin by listening for the main idea. It will be easy to become sidetracked, and you may immediately understand the words and sentences but not the overall purpose. Until you get the overall point, you may misconstrue the facts or put them into the wrong context. Work to fight the natural urge of jumping to conclusions or assuming you know the intended point of the speaker. It's critical to allow people to complete their full ideas, and even better if you can refrain from thinking about your reply while they are still sharing these ideas. It's okay to ask for clarification of a point, but it often helps to wait until they have completed their communication exchange because your question may be answered.

Stop here. Take a minute to think about your reply. At this time, it is advantageous to repeat what you perceived as the purpose of their communication. Sometimes our perceived message does not match the speaker's intended message. We have found that at least 65 percent of the time, what we repeat to a speaker needs to be revised or corrected. It baffles our brains that 65 percent of the time we hear someone speak and we believe we are crystal clear on their message, yet when we share it back with them, we learn we are off the mark. Do we *really* believe that we are incapable of basic human communication? We do, however, believe that when people hear their message projected back to them, it is human nature to revise understanding, include justification, and often soften the message when there is a true effort on the part of the listener to understand the message.

Once you have sustained your attention, engaged in active listening, listened for the main idea, and summarized your perception of the communication intention, it is okay to acknowledge that you want a moment to formulate a reply. As a matter of fact, it is okay to share that you are not ready to reply at the moment. You may request additional time, and this often will work to your advantage.

When we began this practice, we realized that the unintended consequences were amazing. This may be both a bonus and a shock to the speaker. The reality of our world is that people are not used to a leader who is contemplative, so they might be genuinely surprised that they were actually heard and understood.

Below Sandy shares how using process time as a leader has actually worked to her advantage with her staff.

> There have been many times, especially when I was new to a school, that after listening to a teacher pour out their heart for twenty-five minutes, I looked them squarely in the eye and said, "Wow, I need some time with this one." I shared with the staff member that I valued their trust in me and their willingness to seek me out and share their feelings. I told them that I needed a day or two to think through all of the angles of a request. I scheduled a ten- to fifteen-minute follow-up session to touch base with them when I would be able to share my reflections after gathering information and formulating a thoughtful decision. To be honest, I did this because I was new and did not know all the answers. It was my way to gather information and assist my decision-making. It was never part of a grand communication strategy.
>
> But a crazy thing happened. Staff members began to talk. They shared with others that I was thoughtful. That I did not immediately shoot down their ideas. That while they understood my final decision may or may not have been in their favor (often

it was not), they trusted that I had thought about the topic from all angles and that in my follow-up conversation I would justify my reasoning with my "why" and would leave the topic open to being revisited in the future. Almost by accident, I developed a communication strategy that began to define how teachers perceived me as a leader. Because of this, more teachers kept coming, and the communication at the school stayed open and positive.

At some point, though, you will be required to respond to a communication intention. You will give your best response, it will be based on thoughtful contemplation and your evaluation of the facts at a given moment, *and* facts will change. As leaders, somewhere in "principal school," we were led to believe that a decisive leader was a great leader. We were told that people who waffled or changed their opinions were weak and did not make good leaders.

We would like to offer up a different perspective, by way of Jeff Bezos. According to a 2019 *Inc.* article by Tommy Mello, Bezos believes that changing one's mind is a sign of an intelligent leader. The owner of Amazon said that "it's perfectly healthy to have an idea tomorrow that [contradicts] your idea today," and "changing your mind means that you're open to new points of view, new information, and new ideas that contradict or challenge your way of thinking" (Mello 2019).

In a 2012 interview with Basecamp cofounder Jason Fried, Bezos said that "people who tend to be right 'a lot' are the ones who change their minds." Fried noted that Bezos had "observed that the smartest people are constantly revising their understanding, reconsidering a problem they thought they'd already solved. They're open to new points of view, new information, new ideas, contradictions, and challenges to their own way of thinking" (Mello 2019). This allows leaders to continually revise their understanding and reconsider problems they thought they had solved. Mello continued, "At the end of the day, [we] come up with more innovative approaches, and improve upon our existing solutions," when we are brave enough to change our minds.

If You Are Ready to Listen ...

1. Acknowledge the staff member.

2. Ask the staff member to give you a moment to prepare to listen.

3. Actively close your laptop.

4. Adjust your posture or move your seat to sit squarely facing your guest.

5. Breathe slowly and deeply.

6. Physically relax and get comfortable.

7. Ask the speaker if they think it would be important for you to take notes.

8. Listen for the main idea—do not talk.

9. Ask clarifying questions only between sentences.

10. When the speaker has completed their thought, **stop**.

11. Sit for a moment and honor the speaker's ideas and think.

12. Summarize and repeat what you believe you have heard.

13. Respond as needed.

The Importance of Word Choice

Early in our leadership journeys, we learned that language is a powerful tool. We realized that language shapes perceptions and perceptions shape behaviors. There is tremendous power in the way we use language with our staff and what this communicates about our core system of beliefs.

Think of how the terms in Table 9.1 comparing common language and intentional language paint different pictures in the minds of our teachers. As you read this table, think about other words used in education that have a negative connotation and that you think should be utilized more intentionally.

Common Language	Intentional Language
• Achievement gap	• Opportunity gap
• Subgroup	• Specific student group
• But	• And
• Buy-in	• Ownership
• Accountability	• Efficacy

Table 9.1. Intentional Language

As school leaders, it is incumbent upon us to understand the critical importance of our language and how it shapes the perceptions and beliefs of our teachers.

Intentional leaders with Administrator Clarity carefully select their words and use language that casts a light on outcomes rather than opinions. Table 9.2 offers examples of feedback you might give to a teacher.

Instead of Saying This	Try Saying This
That was a great lesson.	Your use of high levels of rigor and questioning was an effective strategy.
Students were engaged and on task.	The way you called upon students X, Y, and Z as nonvolunteers and the fact that each one was able to answer the question was evidence of engagement.
Your classroom walls are inviting.	The walls of your classroom depict student work with teacher feedback and clear expectations about what quality work looks like.
Students seem to really understand the learning target.	I noticed evidence of student learning when I saw _____ .
Do you have any questions about your observation?	What questions do you have specific to your instructional delivery?

Table 9.2. Effective Feedback Samples

It is imperative to understand that our use of language can build teachers up or break them down. It can welcome new ideas or make teachers shy away from sharing.

At one of our schools, we banned the word "but." We began to see that anytime someone came to the table with a new idea, a well-meaning and critically thinking colleague, in an effort to look smart and capable, would follow this idea with "But ..." and then list all the challenges to the given situation. While this input was well-intentioned and purposeful in building on an idea, that is not what it did.

Instead, every "but" got our school leadership team one step further from openness, sharing, and communication. The sharing of ideas became less common. Staff became less willing to open up. When ideas continue to get shot down, people stop sharing. So, with the activity that follows, we began using the rule of "Yes, And."

The "Yes, And" Activity

Our use of language is critical in setting the stage for creating a brave staff, open to sharing new ideas and growing alongside us. We have found that the word "but" can immediately take the wind out of one's sails and leave a speaker reluctant to share ideas again.

Try making a "No Buts" rule at your school and begin with a game of "Yes, And." Yes AND is a common improv "game" that we have adapted because it highlights the importance of positive affirming language. While it seems silly or corny at first, it can transform your school from a place of negativity that lacks safety to a place where people openly build on great ideas.

Here is a step-by-step guide (make sure to model it once before they begin):

1. Place your teachers into partner pairs.

2. Give each pair a scenario (You are planning a party, you are planning a vacation, or you are planning a lesson).

3. Explain the steps:

    a. One person in the pair will start by making the suggestion, like "I want to take a trip."

b. Then the second person will respond to the suggestion, reacting to it with a sentence beginning "Yes, and ..." ("Yes, and I think we should travel by airplane.")

c. Then the first person will respond, reacting to the response with a sentence beginning "Yes, and ..." ("Yes, and let's make sure to pack bathing suits.")

d. Then the second person will respond, reacting to the response with a sentence beginning "Yes, and ..." ("Yes, and we can't forget sunscreen.")

e. They will continue to move forward for a few minutes.

4. Switch up the groups and repeat it again.

5. As with any activity, it's imperative throughout the process that you share exactly why you are having the staff take part in this activity.

The idea to drive home with the teams is that our language matters. Simply contradicting people can leave them feeling dejected and unwilling to share ideas. There is a way to honor others' thoughts without squashing them and continue to build on bigger and greater ideas.

In summary, the chart below highlights many of the concepts we discussed in this chapter about improving your listening skills as a school leader.

How to Improve Your Listening Skills

Listen More, Talk Less	Leading with intention happens when you value the expertise all around you. When talking with a teacher, staff member, or parent, do not respond right away. Wait thirty seconds after the speaker has paused, collect your thoughts, and listen. The answer they are seeking or the idea they have will come out only if we provide the space for them to share it.
Focus on the Goal	Leading with intention means you know your end goal. What do you want your teams to accomplish at the end of the month? Think small. Create a thirty-day plan to achieve it. Plan your staff meeting topics between now and then. Schedule times to check in with teachers along the way. Be intentional in your day-to-day actions.

How to Improve Your Listening Skills

Celebrate Successes	Leading with intention means that you stop to smell the roses along the way. Once your team has achieved a goal or made progress toward it, celebrate! Send a quick email, drop a positive quote in everyone's box, or hand out a fun award. Be intentional about publicly recognizing the hard work that goes into learning (for adults **and** students).
Communicate with Clarity	Leading with intention means you are transparent and clear in your communications with your staff. Never assume that others can read your thoughts. Create a brief weekly newsletter in which you openly share what has been going on in your head regarding instructional practices or the purpose of PLCs. Be authentic. Keep it simple, don't overthink it, but do communicate it.

Chapter Highlights

- Listening is arguably one of the most difficult skills in communication. As humans we spend over 45 percent of our day listening to others. As school leaders, we would argue we spend even more time than that actively engaged in listening, with the expectation of problem-solving.

- As school leaders, it is incumbent upon us to understand the critical importance of our language and how it shapes the perceptions and beliefs of our teachers. Intentional leaders with Administrator Clarity carefully select their words and choose language that focuses on outcomes rather than opinions.

- It is okay to change your mind. Changing one's mind is a sign of an intelligent leader.

Chapter 10

GUIDE TO CHALLENGING CONVERSATIONS AND GIVING FEEDBACK

As we mentioned in previous chapters, the importance of open, honest, and authentic communication and listening is critical in the development of solid relationships with your teachers and staff members. Many times, that simply includes listening, answering questions, and engaging teachers in the work of education. Sometimes, however, the job forces us to have hard conversations. This chapter explores how to have these challenging conversations with success and clarity. We believe that leaders with true Administrator Clarity have perfected the ability to communicate in a way that we have called "intentionally impactful." In this chapter, we discuss four ways that leaders can communicate difficult information and critical feedback. We also share why it is critical that school leaders learn to become intentionally impactful in order to have Administrator Clarity.

The vast majority of us *do not* enjoy conflict, and why would we? Conflict is hard, awkward, and uncomfortable. Effective communication practices can make a leader thrive, and ineffective ones can make a leader struggle to survive. One of the most difficult yet important aspects of communicating with clarity is having difficult conversations.

Balancing communication as a school leader is a delicate art form. You work to connect, reaffirm, and love your people, in the face of an ever-changing and challenging profession; you also balance that with the enormity of making sure students are receiving high-quality instruction every single day. At times, these two goals are at odds. This is especially true in the case of an ineffective teacher.

The Four Types of School Leader Communication

Let's examine the four types of school leader communication. These can best be described by thinking of them as four quadrants, as illustrated in Figure 10.1. The y-axis refers to how empathetic and caring versus aggressive and confrontational a leader is in their communication exchange when delivering challenging information. The x-axis refers to the degree to which someone is direct versus vague in delivering challenging information.

Shockingly, many leaders do not fall into the ideal top right quadrant and spend much of their educational journey struggling to be effective in communicating with their staff. In this chapter, you will find a brief description of the evasively empathetic, directly dictatorial, evasively unkind, and intentionally impactful communication styles, along with a sample of what each of these communication styles looks like in school leadership. We also provide feedback and insight for leaders who fall into each of these categories.

Figure 10.1. School Leader Communication Styles

Communication Style 1: Evasively Empathetic

An evasively empathetic school leader truly cares for their staff. This leader has invested significant time and energy in getting to know each person on the staff. Teachers and staff across campus genuinely enjoy working for this leader. If asked to describe this school leader, teachers would use adjectives such as "kind," "warmhearted," "thoughtful," "compassionate," and "teacher centered."

This leader has also developed such a rapport with their staff that they are no longer willing, or even able, to have challenging, direct conversations focused on student achievement. Or, alternatively, this leader never planned to have challenging conversations with staff, regardless of the relationships developed, and is able to mask some of their overall ineffectiveness with genuine likability.

If you were to ask the staff whether their evasively empathetic school leader was effective at managing the school, many teachers might say yes. Others might report that, while they are uncertain whether this leader truly moved the school forward, the leader certainly did not hurt the school.

District office staff might look at the data and see a slightly different story. Data would likely reveal a fairly stagnant school, or a slight shift downward in performance over time as a result of changes in the demographic without changes happening in instruction. From the district level, among all the forms of ineffective communication, this one is probably the most common and insidious and the least easy to spot when looking from the top down.

If the squeaky wheel gets the oil, nothing at this school squeaks. Happy teachers do not squeak, and even the most challenging teacher on this campus, if asked for their thoughts about this leader, would reply, "Well, they leave me alone and let me do my job." For some teachers, especially those who are less effective, being "left alone" is equated with effective leadership.

District superintendents and leaders may be duped into believing that these schools are run by effective leaders. To some extent, they are. Very few teachers leave this campus, and there is always a line to get in and work for these leaders. They have developed a rapport with their staff, which is the first step in effective communication. If this leader is able to parlay their relationships and overcome their fear, they can take their leadership to the next level and communicate in a manner that is effective and able to move the school forward.

The leadership problem with this type of communication is in what happens when you care but do not challenge. A leader like this doles out praise to everyone they encounter. Since this leader is all about the positive, often their praise is weak and lacks specificity. Often, this leader does not possess the knowledge to effectively evaluate instruction, so they hide behind being likable and popular with their staff.

Of all the ineffective communication styles among school leaders, this one is the most common. We surmise this is because, by and large, those who go into education crave connection. We genuinely see and care about people. It is much easier to maintain relationships and maintain the status quo by not addressing areas of weakness and need for growth. Challenging conversations, the ones that push schools forward, are not always soft and do not always connect people. Evasively empathetic school leaders focus on their connections and avoid having challenging conversations. As a result, they often fail to move their school forward at the pace that could be possible, or even at all. Sometimes these leaders can, in extreme circumstances, have a difficult conversation, but by and large, these are avoided and the school suffers.

This Communication Style in Practice

Mr. Lockwood has been teaching at Wuthering Heights Elementary School for three years. The new school leader, Ms. Heathcliff, started at this school a year ago. Mr. Lockwood is a good and solid man, a single father whose wife left him after an affair several years ago. Ms. Heathcliff knows the story from district rumors because Mr. Lockwood's wife also worked in the district. Ms. Heathcliff spent her first year getting to know Mr. Lockwood. He was a stand-up and go-to guy. If there was a tough kid, a kid other teachers did not want, Mr. Lockwood would take that student and never complain. At face value, Mr. Lockwood seemed like a dream teacher.

But he was not. It took only two minutes in Mr. Lockwood's classroom to see that students were not learning. When you walked in, you were more likely to be hit with a spitball than to see a hand raised. Test scores from his benchmarks were abysmal. On a happy note, parents never complained. Mr. Lockwood was everyone's best friend, the person each of them wanted for their neighbor. Any school leader would be able to recognize that Mr. Lockwood was in need of coaching and support.

Ms. Heathcliff knew and understood the challenges that Mr. Lockwood had experienced over the past three years. It was clear to him, as it was to every other teacher on campus, that his classroom was out of control. When his PLC team finally walked into her office and put their foot down, she stopped and listened. They shared with her that he was not pulling his weight as a teammate. He did not seem to be following the curriculum, and the lack of rules in his classroom was impacting the entire grade level. Ms. Heathcliff listened. She feigned genuine concern, told the team that this was not acceptable, and then told them the situation would be remedied. The teachers left her office confident the situation would be dealt with; they truly cared for Ms. Heathcliff and she for them.

A week went by as Ms. Heathcliff was avoiding the chance to speak with Mr. Lockwood. When the opportunity finally presented itself during an observation evaluation review, Ms. Heathcliff asked Mr. Lockwood how things were going with his grade-level team. He reported that things were great. She then asked him about the lesson he was delivering to his students and he recounted a story of an appreciative parent and dove into how much those little victories had helped him get through the struggles in his personal life during the past few years.

Ms. Heathcliff quickly deleted her coaching comments on the evaluation, thanked him for his dedication to his students, and dismissed him from the office. He cheerfully went on his way, proud of his great evaluation and unaware of the storm brewing in his PLC group.

Meanwhile, his PLC team was confident that this evaluation conference, which they all knew he was having, would be the time the hammer would be dropped. When he breezed into their meeting as clueless and ineffective as he was before, his colleagues could not help but make this situation more toxic. They stopped inviting him to PLC meetings and often wondered why he did not take their leader's feedback and at least try to improve.

This school leader, while widely adored by staff at Wuthering Heights Elementary School, has unintentionally divided the school as a result of her communication style. Although the staff does not know this, her inability to hold all staff to the same high standards has begun to rip apart the fabric of the school. Staff are turning on one another, and much of this is related to the school leader's inability to have hard conversations.

The evasively empathetic leadership style is best summed up as either giving praise that is not specific enough to help the person understand what was good or giving criticism that is sugarcoated and unclear.

Feedback for Growth

From a young age, we are taught to be "nice" and that if we do not have something nice to say, we should not say anything. In truth, it is not a bad impulse to protect people's feelings, but it provides only short-lived protection.

Intentionally impactful leaders realize that it is their own feelings they are protecting, not those of their staff. If you cannot be direct with your staff, you may be setting people up for bigger failure, and more hurt feelings, later. Convincing yourself that "it will all work out" absent your intervention is simply denial.

Five Things You Can Do Today to Grow in This Area

1. Start small. Schedule one person per week for whom you will provide critical feedback.

2. Prepare notes about one or two items you are looking to see change.

3. When giving critical feedback, chunk it into one to two pieces of feedback per session.

4. Ask when you can come in to see the implementation of your feedback.

5. Celebrate implementation.

Communication Style 2: Directly Dictatorial

A directly dictatorial school leader knows how to make a point. This leader has a clear and concise understanding of what good instruction, great PLCs, and great schools look like.

This leader has invested significant time and energy in understanding the four questions of the PLCs and how schools go from good to great and has a tremendous capacity to lead. When speaking with the superintendent, this leader comes across as someone who clearly knows how to run a school. They can cite Hattie's effect sizes the way others recite the Pledge of Allegiance.

Yet this leader's one fatal flaw has gotten them involved in more than a few challenging situations and has earned them the label of micromanager. The problem with this school leader is that while they clearly know how to manage a school, they know nothing about managing people. They have failed to form genuine connections, and so when they make requests of their staff, staff members question their motives and often fear for their jobs. While this leader is able to get a level of ritualized compliance, it is likely that the district leadership views them as somewhat of a know-it-all because of their inability to connect on a human level.

If you were to ask the staff whether their directly dictatorial leader was effective at managing the school, many teachers might say yes. They might share that they were always provided with clear and high expectations and they knew well what their leader needed from them. They might also report that at times they were fearful, they lacked basic job security, and they always felt as if they were walking on eggshells. This leader is clear but not kind; the leader's praise does not feel sincere, and criticism is not delivered kindly. Dictatorially direct leaders are also noted for their brutal honesty or "front stabbing." They often lead with a phrase such as "Let me be really candid with you" and then follow with words like "Your data doesn't lie, and you are failing our students" or "No one likes you."

This Communication Style in Practice

Mr. Lockwood had been teaching at Wuthering Heights Elementary School for three years. The new school leader, Ms. Brontë, started at this school a year ago. She has gone into his classroom several times. Each time she leaves, she sends a follow-up email. Here is her most recent communication:

Mr. Lockwood,

I came into your classroom today from 11:45 to 12:15. I observed the following:

- *Fifteen of eighteen students were off task.*
- *There was no posted objective.*
- *You provided no scaffolding or supports for your English learners.*
- *You provided no access to higher-order thinking for your gifted learners.*
- *You did not appropriately integrate technology into your lesson.*
- *Students were released to independent practice with no check for mastery.*
- *Work posted in the classroom was four weeks old and lacked feedback.*

As a result of this observation, you are hereby put on a PIP—a performance improvement plan.

Exhausted and dejected after reading her latest email, Mr. Lockwood sat down with a group of teachers at lunch. He told them of his awful classroom observation, of how he was a failure as a teacher, and of how he believed that Ms. Bronte must be out to get him. The other teachers listened.

While they knew Mr. Lockwood had areas in which to grow as a teacher, they could not help but take pity on him and the challenging situation that he had been put in. Word began to spread around the campus that Ms. Bronte's informal pop-ins were anything but informal and she was using these observations as a way to fire teaching staff. The level of anxiety increased across the campus every time teachers heard her high heels clomping down the halls.

Feedback for Growth

Often, school leaders adopt a directly dictatorial style because they are so focused on the work that they have forgotten there is a human being doing the work. Sadly, in its extreme form, leaders who publicly degrade people or give them the cold shoulder also fall into this category. The vast majority of school leaders who fall into this category are results-driven and smart and know what quality instruction looks like. Often, they do care on some basic level but have failed to learn how to show it.

Intentionally impactful leaders realize that clarity is important and it is kind to be clear with your staff, but this must also be coupled with a genuine belief in them and desire to connect with them.

Five Things You Can Do Today to Grow in This Area

1. Schedule a fifteen-minute getting-to-know-you meeting with every new hire.
2. Provide regular opportunities for your teachers to see you (office hours).
3. Ask questions and keep notes.
4. Celebrate birthdays and special occasions of your staff.
5. Drop notes of recognition and appreciation for your staff.

Communication Style 3: Evasively Unkind

An evasively unkind school leader is one who neither cares nor challenges. This is a leader who gives praise that is nonspecific and insincere or criticism that is neither clear nor kind. These school leaders are not willing to challenge directly. Their approach creates a toxic school culture consisting of backstabbing, political, and passive-aggressive behavior that breaks a school at its very core. These leaders give praise and criticism that is insincere because they are too focused on being liked.

An evasively unkind school leader does not care for their staff. They invest no time or energy in getting to know staff members. They also have little to no ability to create and implement clear and actionable goals for staff. Teachers and staff across campus genuinely dislike working for this leader. If asked about the school leader, teachers might use adjectives such as "toxic," "unkind," "mean," "pushy," "detached," "uninvolved," "vague," and "awful."

This leader has not developed any rapport with the staff, and the teachers do not come to them for guidance or support. Few if any conversations about student achievement take place on this campus because most time is spent complaining about the job, complaining about the students, or complaining about the leadership.

If you were to ask the staff whether their evasively unkind school leader was effective at managing the school, nearly everyone would agree this was an awful environment for staff and students alike.

The district office staff are typically well aware of the ineffectiveness of this school leader. It is clear from school data that performance is trending downward. Staff surveys indicate an unhappy staff, and complaints up to the district level are frequent. From the district level, of all of the styles of ineffective communication, the evasively unkind style is by far the most detrimental to the performance of a school and probably easiest to spot when looking from the top down.

Among all of the ineffective communication styles in school leadership, this one is the most toxic. When people feel neither guided nor led, they have little motivation. When a leader does not genuinely see and care about people, it is very hard to have followers. This, coupled with a lack of direction and clarity for the job at hand, is a combination that can bring a school crashing down.

This Communication Style in Practice

Mr. Charlotte is a new school leader at Wuthering Heights Elementary School. He typically shows up for his school day fifteen to twenty minutes after his teachers. He knows many of his teachers by name, but not all. When he first started, teachers popped into his office to get to know him and his vision for the school. Most reported that he seemed distracted or uninterested in sharing a conversation with them.

When asked about his goals for the school, he throws out some motivational phrases about being "the best" and keeping the school "great" but does not have specific actionable ideas about how that will be done. When he gives praise, it is always nonspecific and typically comes at the same time as a request. Even his feedback on improvement seems related more to something he overheard the teacher say about him than to student achievement or the school overall.

When teachers walk by his office, most days the door is closed. His secretary has reported overhearing him bad-mouthing teachers and students to colleagues across the district on telephone calls, sometimes even making fun of students because of their buck teeth or minor lisp.

Feedback for Growth

These leaders are often simply overwhelmed or ill-suited for the leadership role that is required of them. If this is an area you are struggling to grow in, the advice below may help you in this area of communication.

1. Speak to your supervisor about getting a mentor within your district.
2. Provide regular opportunities for your teachers to meet with you (office hours).
3. Seek out professional development training on concepts such as coaching, PLCs, and the feedback cycle.
4. Practice giving out one piece of specific, actionable praise and one piece of specific, actionable critical feedback each day.
5. Stop and listen to your staff without talking. Just make an effort to understand what they are feeling and what they need.

Communication Style 4: Intentionally Impactful

Intentionally impactful school leaders care personally for their staff and address directly any concerns that may arise. Intentionally impactful communication honors the idea that there is inherent emotional labor in caring for a team, and it is undervalued but essential. Intentionally impactful school leaders recognize that they are responsible for guiding their team to achieve results. They understand that their duties can be classified as follows:

- Expectation setting (giving feedback, setting expectations)
- Capacity building (finding and inspiring the right people for each position at the school)
- End results (inspiring staff to meet goals and work together in order improve outcomes for student achievement)

Intentionally impactful communication recognizes that good school leaders must develop relationships with the people who report directly to them. Authority will not substitute for relationships.

To be effective in the realm of intentionally impactful communication, school leaders must recognize that the two key elements of communication are their level of personal caring and their ability to directly challenge.

As a school leader, if you care for your staff and they trust that you care for them, they are more likely to take your feedback with the assumption of positive intentions. In addition, when they experience struggles and challenges, they will trust that they can come to you for support and feedback.

Intentionally impactful school leaders provide guidance that is both kind and clear. As Table 10.1 shows, intentionally impactful leaders do not worry about keeping things "professional." Instead an intentionally impactful leader trusts that by being their most authentic self, they will build the best rapport with their staff.

What Intentionally Impactful School Leaders Do	What This Looks Like
Solicit feedback	• Intentionally impactful school leaders can start by asking staff to give them feedback. Soliciting guidance, especially criticism, is not something you do once and then check off your list—it is something you must do daily.
	• It needs to happen in the little one- to two-minute conversations, not in meetings you have to add to your calendar. It is something to be conscious of, not something to schedule. It will feel strange at first, but once you get into the habit, it will feel weird not to do it.
Master the "one-on-one in one" conversation	• As a school leader, you should grab a clipboard and walk the campus.
	• Make sure to have a one-on-one conversation with every teacher that lasts at least one minute.
	• It helps to start with a simple question that you ask every employee. This can transform into giving each staff member feedback specific to an area of focus for the school (e.g., formative assessment or the feedback cycle).

What Intentionally Impactful School Leaders Do	What This Looks Like
Iterate	• Intentionally impactful school leaders embrace the iterative process. Once you have opened up to feedback from your staff and shown them you care, then you can give clear, concise, and targeted feedback. When they have implemented the feedback, build in time to revise your process and evaluate their implementation.
	• What worked well that you need to continue?
	• What did not work that needs to be stopped?
	• What new practices related to this area need to start?

Table 10.1. Qualities of an Intentionally Impactful School Leader

Chapter Highlights

- Leader communication styles fall into one of four quadrants.

- Evasively empathetic school leaders truly care for their staff. These leaders have invested significant time and energy in getting to know each person on the staff. Teachers and staff across campus genuinely enjoy working for them. Despite the time spent to build this relationship, the staff at their schools often remain unclear on their overall goals and expectations.

- Directly dictatorial school leaders know how to make a point. They have a clear and concise understanding of what good instruction, great PLCs, and great schools look like, but they can struggle with establishing rapport with staff.

- Evasively unkind school leaders neither care nor challenge. They are leaders who give praise that is nonspecific and insincere or criticism that is neither clear nor kind.

- Intentionally impactful school leaders both care personally for their staff and address directly any concerns that may arise. They solicit feedback, have mastered the one-on-one, and understand the iterative process.

Chapter 11

THE ROLE OF RECOGNITION AS FEEDBACK

This chapter focuses on providing examples of and rationales for systems that recognize and communicate to teachers when expectations are met or exceeded via clear and consistent feedback cycles and recognition. Research regularly points out that recognition and celebrations of staff performance increase productivity and are an essential component of the feedback loop. When staff are recognized and celebrated for their impact and professional growth, success blossoms, ultimately leading to student achievement (Jackson 2022).

What makes *you* feel valued within your organization? How do you know you are meeting the mark?

There has been a lot of fanfare over the past ten years about the importance of feedback from school leaders. While we fundamentally agree that feedback by administrators can be an effective tool for school leaders, we also believe that this strategy often falls short of being effective, as a result of poor implementation.

All too often, teachers and administrators alike share that they have never received feedback, whether constructive or celebratory, in their entire career (Louis et al. 2010). While they believe that they meet the expectations set forth by school or district leadership, there is no recognition of this accomplishment, nor is there feedback along their path toward the common goal. This lack of recognition and celebration can have negative implications, including but not limited to a decrease in teachers' persistence through challenges that arise and an increase in teachers not feeling valued for the effort, energy, and heart that they put into their own professional learning and growth as they stretch themselves to meet the diverse needs of their students.

Systems that celebrate teachers when expectations are met or exceeded via clear and consistent feedback cycles are hubs where students excel academically. For school leaders, with so many things to get done daily, recognition of others often gets overlooked or bypassed with something more pressing and urgent. School leaders who practice Administrator Clarity recognize that feedback is a critical component of clarity. How can one have true clarity of expectations without specific, actionable feedback?

We are here to tell you to *pause*, *breathe*, and *celebrate*. Despite the daily challenges that come your way, pausing to provide recognition feeds your soul and leads to student *and* adult learning and growth.

We encourage you to try this:

- Create a reasonable plan for classroom visits (try to visit 10 percent of classrooms per day—these may be divided among the administrative team).

- Go into the classroom with the lens of achieving your school-wide goal—what evidence you might be looking for to support that the school is making progress toward the agreed-upon school-wide goal.

- Articulate to the teacher what school-wide goal you are looking for during your visits. School leaders who lead with clarity never use classroom visits as a "gotcha" moment but rather are constantly seeking to improve specific practices that impact student achievement. Leaders who lead with Administrator Clarity also know that what gets monitored gets done.

- Create a framework for what you will be providing feedback on based on a shared instructional framework that aligns with the school-wide goal.

- Provide immediate feedback, framed with specific information, genuine wonderings, and a nonevaluative invitation to further dialogue.

John Hattie's research on Visible Learning can give school leaders a lot of topics on which they can focus their attention. These make a great jumping-off point to align and couple with school-wide program improvement goals as you circulate the campus.

We want you to know that this act of recognition and celebration is fairly simple and easy to implement. Recognizing growth can take the form of a note left in a teacher's classroom, a staff newsletter article about a grade level's data highlighting student growth, or even an old-fashioned face-to-face conversation sharing these sentiments.

However you choose to recognize the hard work of others and celebrate their accomplishments along the way, the feedback must be (1) specific and intentional, (2) genuine and sincere, and (3) prompt and timely. Follow the guidelines below to have the intended impact.

Specific and Intentional. **Your recognition of progress and/or celebration of the process should focus on the instructional practices and learning that are aligned with your school-wide goal.**

Rather Than Say: "Your lesson was really great. I noticed your students talking and explaining their thinking during your math lesson."

Say: "I observed one of your English learners using the language patterns embedded in your math lesson on adding fractions. I heard her explaining to her partner how she arrived at her answer using one of the sentence frames available to her. This was an effective way to support her mathematical communication."

Genuine and Sincere. **Your recognition of progress and/or celebration of the process should come from the heart and from what you actually observe happening.**

Rather Than Say: "I can tell you are working hard with your class. Keep up the great work!"

Say: "I want to let you know I see how hard you are working to ensure your students are making academic growth in their mathematical communication. I've observed your small-group intervention lessons, and it is evident that your English learners have the appropriate support to communicate their mathematical thinking. Thank you for being on this journey with us and making a positive impact."

Prompt and Timely. Your recognition of progress and/or celebration of the process should be prompt and be within an appropriate window of time.

Rather Than Say: "Last month, when I came into your classroom, I observed the students were very engaged in your lesson on adding fractions."

Say: "Today, when I visited your classroom, I observed students who were participating in the lesson by engaging in dialogue with their partners."

***

At one of the schools where Marine worked, her administrator often left notes that focused on feedback and praise. The principal visited classrooms and left notes that provided recognition of the instructional moves she saw that were aligned with the school's vision of increased structured student talk within content-area lessons. The administrator left these notes in the classroom upon her exit. Here, Marine describes the impact these notes had on her as a teacher.

> One way I grew most as a teacher was by receiving effective feedback and praise from one of my administrators. Whenever my admin walked through, it wasn't about being evaluative. It was about support, acknowledgment, and recognition of hard work and student progress (small or big). One way she did that was by using these notes every time she walked through. She wrote about what she saw, what she heard, and any wonderings she had about what was happening during her time in our classrooms. I loved how personal these notes were and the positive effect they had on my teaching style.

Marine's experience should resonate with every school leader. The effort on the part of the administrator was minimal, yet the impact was profound. This particular strategy to recognize and celebrate teachers' progress toward the school's goals serves two purposes. It gets you into classrooms, witnessing the teaching and learning happening on a daily basis, *and* it offers you an opportunity to celebrate what you see. Often, we walk in and out of classrooms making mental notes about what we observe, but rarely do those observational notes reach the intended recipient. By providing communication that incorporates feedback *and* recognition, we enter into the feedback loop with our teachers and invite them into the ongoing dialogue on teaching and learning we hope to foster within our school cultures. Use the sentence stems in Table 11.1 to help begin that dialogue.

Asking clarifying questions	1. So what I am hearing you say is …
	2. May I repeat back to you what I perceive as your intended message?
	3. Let me see if I understand correctly.
	4. What makes you feel the way that you feel?
	5. Can you share more about …
Celebrating	1. What is going well in your classroom?
	2. What do you feel was the best part of that lesson?
	3. What are you most proud of this school year?
Validating	1. I can see that you're trying to …
	2. I was excited to see you take a risk and try …
	3. In doing (x), you were effective in meeting your goal of (y).
Questioning	1. What do you think would happen if you changed …
	2. Help me understand more about your reasoning when you …
	3. If you changed (x), what do you think the impact may be?
	4. I am fascinated with (x), please tell me more.
Consulting	1. What do you think about … ?
	2. Would you like to visit other classrooms with me? Where do you think you would be able to gather the most information?
	3. Would you be open to trying "x" and inviting me back in to see how it is going?

Table 11.1. Sentence Stems That You Can Use on Your Campus

Teachers and staff members may have difficulty detecting meaning when the school leader is imprecise or lacks intention and direction. Table 11.2 will help you read into the communication and bring the conversation back on target by honoring the teacher or staff member's perspective and then refocusing on feedback.

Teacher/Staff Member Comment	Align with Value Set	Refocus on Constructive Feedback
"The students are out of control in the cafeteria. They don't raise their hand to throw out their trash, and they constantly disrespect the adults. They make me crazy."	"What I am hearing is that student behavior is important to you and you value order within our various school settings."	"I can work with the deans to reestablish and review the behavioral expectations with our student population. Would you mind meeting with them to review these expectations and see if anything needs to be added?"
"PLCs and staff meetings are an unproductive waste of time."	"You value fair and valuable time as a team, which impacts your job and student learning; is that right?"	"Let's review school-wide norms for PLCs and staff meetings, and help me understand where we are falling short so that we can improve in this area."

Table 11.2. Honoring Other Perspectives[1]

---

1 Adapted from Robert J. Garmston, "Collaborative Culture: Raise the Level of Conversation by Using Paraphrasing as a Listening Skill," *Journal of Staff Development* 29, no. 2 (Spring 2008): 53–54.

Celebrate

Celebrate your staff's focus along the way! Use the template in Figure 11.1 to drop them a note and let them know you see them and their efforts. Highlight what you see in the classroom in your weekly newsletter, staff messages, or school social media pages. Share the learning process with all!

Principal Pop-In

Thank you for allowing me to pop in and see you and your classroom today. I always enjoy the time I spend watching you engage in the art and science of educating. Below are a few notes from my visit!

I saw: [One effective practice you saw]

I heard: [One effective practice you heard]

I want to celebrate: [One thing you saw that you thought was great]

As always, thank you for letting me come by, and thanks for doing amazing things for our kids!

Figure 11.1. Principal Pop-In Template

Celebrate their successes at the end. Be intentional and clear about what you have observed throughout this process. Highlight strengths and share them publicly. Praise the process that led to the outcomes rather than just the assessment scores.

> ## *Chapter Highlights*
>
> - Research regularly points out that recognition and celebration of staff performance increase productivity and are an essential component of the feedback loop. When staff are recognized and celebrated for their impact and professional growth, success blossoms, ultimately leading to student achievement.
>
> - When delivered, feedback should be targeted and specific, genuine, and prompt.

Clarity of Sustainability

Chapter 12

THE IMPORTANCE OF DEVELOPING A SUCCESSION PLAN

Starting with the End in Mind

School leadership is not all about action. The very best school leaders understand that when they leave, if their presence is not missed, then their impact was not felt. They also desire that their schools thrive and flourish years after they have departed the campus. This chapter describes how to create an intentional succession plan, from your very first days on campus to your last, so that student achievement will continue to be front and center long after you have left the school.

Sometimes, life is what happens when we are busy making other plans. The first day we walk onto our new campus and are handed the keys, the last thing on our mind is what will happen on our last day. The shocking and stark reality is that at some point that last day comes, whether we like it or not. How we have prepared for it, since day one, frames the future success of our school and the impact of our legacy. As school leaders, we must begin with that end in mind. Developing a succession plan *before* a leadership change will help schools transition effectively and avoid the pitfalls that often come with such a change. As school leaders, we really need to think about succession planning not as a periodic event triggered by our departure but instead as a systematic investment of time and energy into a pipeline of potential future leaders.

School leaders who feel the need to micromanage and keep all of the knowledge to themselves often find themselves frustrated and struggling when change happens. Since they have not built up the capacity of those around them, when they leave the school, so much of what was working at the school then leaves with them as they walk out the door.

Step 1: Build a Team of Rockstars and Superstars

When we first began as principals, we thought that the key to staffing our school was to fill it with what Sinan Ata referred to as "Superstars" in his 2019 article on the Medium website. You know who we are referring to: those staff members, eager to be promoted, who give 110 percent of themselves to their jobs—day in and day out. We thought that these people, destined to be the future leaders of the school, were the ones we should hire and build our schools around.

Reading his article helped us understand what we were missing when we limited ourselves to hiring for Superstar status.

According to Ata, and with some feedback from executives at Apple, there are two types of standouts in any organization, and a successful organization (or school) will work to properly balance both of them. If we think of these as part of a quadrant, we already know clearly we do *not* want people with low performance capability, so, taking them out of the equation, we are left with two types of high performers.

Ata goes on to divide those high performers into two additional groupings: those with steep and slow growth trajectories. He calls those with a steep growth trajectory "Superstars" and those with a slow growth trajectory "Rockstars." The example that follows is a good way to think about the Superstars in our schools.

> You all know that second-year teacher who comes to your school and immediately pushes to be on the leadership team. She has enrolled in her master's program, and she is single-handedly spearheading three school initiatives. She is a typical Superstar. Some principals and district leaders frown on these highly

motivated people pushing for promotion, thinking they need to "put in their time" or "wait their turn." As leaders, we must remind ourselves to appreciate those who are highly motivated to get a promotion and are going to push the limits of learning and experimentation to get a better job, inside or outside. Our schools need people like this to take leadership roles and keep their motivations high.

As school leaders, we have been guilty of seeking out Superstars and forsaking other solid employees, such as the other type of high-performing employee, who Ata refers to as Rockstars. Rockstars are all about stability (hence the "rock" in their name)—so they're the ones who would not especially benefit from a promotion. Unlike Superstars, Rockstars are on a more gradual growth trajectory. These are the people who are the source of stability in your school. They were there five years before you came in as school leader and will likely be there five years after you leave.

These are the teachers on your staff who you thought had a lot more potential, but you are surprisingly happy with what they are doing. Even though they are top performers, their dream is just keeping the job they have and doing it for many years. Well, these are typical Rockstars. They have rock-solid knowledge and expertise but are content where they are at the moment. There are many others with less expertise and success taking higher seats, but they choose to stay where they are happy.

As school administrators, we have had to remind ourselves that it is not about choosing one of two groups; rather, it is about finding the balance, because your school needs both Rockstars and Superstars. It is also helpful for you as a school leader to understand that depending on where your school is and what initiatives you may be launching, you may have a different need in terms of recruitment and hiring. This next example highlights the situational need for Superstars and Rockstars.

Lisa has just been charged with the responsibility of opening a new charter school. While the projection for her year one launch is roughly 1,000 students, over the next three to five years her school is projected to grow to 5,000 students. As she completes recruitment and hiring, her needs will be different from those of a traditional principal of a long-established school with stagnant or declining enrollment. Lisa may want to think of her school more as a start-up company and create a Superstar-heavy team, knowing that she will quickly be promoting many of her team members into leadership roles. The projected accelerated growth makes it critical for her to have people on her team eager to move up and into new leadership roles. However, in five to seven years, as growth tapers off, Lisa will want to consider looking for Rockstars, those employees eager to perform at high levels but not eager to move into different roles. These employees will provide the stability her school will need at that time to continue on a path of sustained success.

Step 2: Intentionally Create a Diverse Team

It is not enough to bring "good" people to your team. It is critical to bring diverse people to your team. We are all always looking to create the strongest teams and to bring people into our leadership circles who we see possess that Superstar quality. However, at times, we can be myopic in creating our leadership teams if we are not intentional about inviting voices to our table that may be different from our own. It is more critical than ever that we create seats at our table for diverse team members.

In December of 2020, Simon Sinek delivered a TED Talk, titled What Diversity and Inclusion Is REALLY About. In this TED TALK he shared the idea that, as individuals, we all have on blinders. We can only see things from our own perspective. It is when we come together with a common cause or a shared vision that our view broadens and we can see and recognize things that we never could've seen on our own. He asserts that this is precisely why the best companies are diverse: they have diverse thinking.

In his February 2021 article for the Nonprofit Leadership Center, Christopher Johnson outlined eight key concepts for creating diverse teams. Seven of those concepts, including the key concepts of diversity, equity, and inclusion's application within the school, are summarized below,[2] with additional applications appropriate to school leadership.

1. Cultivating a culture of diversity, equity, and inclusion (DEI) is everyone's responsibility.

Summary: Diversity, equity, and inclusion must be modeled and embraced by the school leader. Principals who truly model DEI know this and never lose sight of embedding these values in the fabric of their school's culture.

Application to Leading a School: In recent years, schools have started having discussions about the concepts of diversity, equity, and inclusion, even bringing in directors of DEI at the district level. Although school districts must create greater accountability for and focus on this work, a single department or position is not a substitute for building and cultivating an authentic culture of DEI.

2. No marginalized population is more important than another.

Summary: Principals who authentically embrace DEI understand that there are many marginalized populations within our schools. DEI issues include race, sexual orientation, gender, disabilities, and more. Inclusive school leaders advocate for all students.

Application to Leading a School: School leaders need to make it part of their daily routine to walk the campus and have the conversations to understand all of the unique populations that make up their school.

3. One person's experience does not discredit another's experience.

Summary: As an inclusive leader, we must understand that we all have different life experiences, even if we come from similar populations. It can be easy to make assumptions about experiences, but true inclusiveness means waiting and allowing each person to share their unique experience.

Application to Leading a School: Leaders who are authentically committed to DEI know they have a responsibility to listen and hear people—to understand others' experiences and not question their validity because they cannot relate to that experience or problem.

---

2 Adapted from Christopher Johnson, "Leaders Who Authentically Embrace Diversity, Equity & Inclusion Believe These 8 Things" (Tampa, FL: Nonprofit Leadership Center, February 22, 2021), https://nlctb.org/tips/inclusive-leadership/?gclid=CjwKCAjwqeWKBhB -FEiwABo_XBlMmBZufyVn5LhhhYXFR3OyECU0KPoxsbqF_Tt4cM4WqAtFgBy8pGxoC84 -AQAvD_BwE.

4. Words do matter.

Summary: Principals who authentically embrace DEI know that "diversity," "equity," "equality," and "inclusion" are not synonyms of one another. They seek to broaden their understanding of these concepts both for themselves and in order to support others.

Application to Leading a School: Within the school system, cultivating diversity means making sure everyone is represented on the school campus. Inclusion involves asking the people on the campus who are different from us to provide feedback and input on school-wide decision-making. In our schools, we may see people of color, women, and those with disabilities invited to the planning table; that's diversity. But they do not always have a voice. Inclusion requires us to invite those voices in, valuing them and ensuring they shape a strategy or plan. The concepts of equality and equity are often misunderstood. Many think that providing everyone with the same things (equality) will achieve this goal. In reality, it is equity that matters. This means that everyone is provided with support in order to participate on a level playing field.

5. Actions mean more than words.

Summary: Principals may fear that they will make a mistake in this area and that their words will be offensive.

Application to Leading a School: According to Johnson, recognizing that mistake is not what is wrong; it is not doing anything about it moving forward, once you are aware of it, that is a problem. Inclusive principals can reflect on their actions and behaviors and identify how to take action to mitigate them.

6. It starts by meeting people where they are.

Summary: Inclusive leaders understand that different people are at various places along the continuum in their journey. Introducing enhancements to an organization's culture takes time and conversations

Application to Leading a School: Authentically committed leaders identify where people are and create safe spaces for dialogue and engagement. They have the courage to have uncomfortable conversations with their staff, board members, and partners about these issues and are not afraid to raise challenging questions.

7. There is no finish line.

Summary: School leaders who have made DEI their goal understand that there is no end point in this work. Rather, there is a constant revisiting and reevaluation of progress.

Application to Leading a School: Inclusive leaders consistently try to improve when it comes to embracing DEI—working on it, prioritizing their focus on it, and ultimately building and strengthening a long-term culture of DEI to change the future.

Step 3: Identify Key Areas and Interested Employees, and Assess Them against Capabilities

As a school leader, if you have set a clear mission and vision for your school and made sure to impart them to your staff, this will assist in your legacy lasting long past the day you exit the school doors. Developing an internal pipeline is something every school leader should plan—and then approach team members who may be good candidates. If you do this, even if someone is brought in from the outside, the fundamental positive impacts on the school will carry on in your absence.

The stark reality is that although our schools' future cannot be predicted, it can be invented. We can shape it through leadership succession planning. Change is inevitable, and it can be disruptive. How successfully our schools adapt to demographic shifts, manage economic swings, and adjust to cultural tides depends largely upon the strength and continuity of leadership.

It is important to remember that a leader helps others to find their path. When school leaders empower their teachers, it pays off in dividends in school culture, influence, vision, and succession planning. It begins with remembering that this is collaborative work that we do.

To begin this process, you must follow a few simple steps.

Meet Teachers Where They Are

As school leaders, one way we can fail in building capacity is by pulling teachers out of their worlds and into ours. Wise leaders who are able to develop their staff flip this model. They immerse themselves in their teachers' worlds. School leaders seeking teacher leaders will learn much more about their staff by immersing themselves in the meetings held by their teams, by quietly listening to their challenges, and by seeking to understand what is going on in their worlds. School leaders should strive to push into the staff meetings and team meetings to get to know their teacher leaders within their areas of expertise.

Redefine School Leadership Roles

Often school administrators, desperate to engage teachers in conversations about moving the school forward, invite teachers to join in the leadership capacity by stepping into the role of a department chair or teacher leader. Not surprisingly, some teachers have shied away from assuming leadership positions quite simply because they do not see this as the job they were hired to do. In addition, assuming the role of a department chair often feels less about leadership and more about additional work. Tasks such as ordering supplies and tracking expenditures—often relegated to these roles—do not really work to push a school vision and mission forward.

As a school leader you should seek to create leadership opportunities and make those opportunities valuable learning experiences for your staff members. Assigning out a managerial task will no more inspire a teacher leader than it will inspire you. It may backfire and appear that you are passing off your work. Instead give them passion projects and projects of value.

Managerial tasks do not stir the blood of dedicated teachers. They desire to solve complex problems that they are faced with in the classroom. School administrators must capture their attention to lead in these areas.

Seek Out Strengths and Hidden Experts and Create Roles

We have all been guilty of wondering how we can get those Superstar and Rockstar teachers' qualities to rub off on the others. Sadly, high performance is not always contagious. Sometimes as school leaders we spend so much time trying to solve other people's problems for them that we forget to bring others' ideas, opinions, and questions into the conversation.

In education, as leaders, we need to remember that time is currency. Most teachers will tend to devote their spare time to their students because working with kids is their primary passion and their comfort area.

As school leaders, it is incumbent upon us to work and nudge teachers in new directions. Teacher leaders must be made aware that these opportunities exist and must be encouraged to step up and into these new roles. We must carve out a time and place where teachers can emerge as leaders. The strongest school administrators, who have the most lasting impact, begin their first day on the job watching and determining with whom, where, and how they can develop teacher leaders and create pathways for building capacity among staff members.

Develop and Implement Succession and Knowledge Transfer Plans, and Evaluate Effectiveness

The best time to prepare your school for your eventual departure is long before you believe that you will be leaving. Even if you believe that you will be on your campus for many years, the reality is that you do not know. The best thing that you can do for the present and future state of your school is to build capacity within your team now.

You may be familiar with the amazing leadership book *The Multiplier Effect: Tapping the Genius inside Our Schools* by Liz Wiseman, Lois Allen, and Elise Foster. The idea proposed in this book is that the single most effective thing we can do as leaders is realize that we do not have a monopoly on leadership. The more we push ourselves to recognize areas in which we can train and build up others, the more effective we will be.

Remember That Your Leadership Directly Impacts Employee Retention

In an article by the National Association of Secondary School Principals (NASSP) and the National Association of Elementary School Principals (NAESP) (2013), a 2010 Gates Foundation study was cited that stated supportive leadership is the most critical factor impacting retention. The NAASP article went on to cite a North Carolina study in 2009 that also found that school leadership is the most relevant measure of working conditions.

It goes without saying the culture is the catalyst for nearly everything else that we do on our campuses and this includes working conditions and employee retention. As school leaders, to build a successful school, we must retain great teachers. We can retain great teachers by sharing that leadership and empowering and inspiring those on our staff.

Chapter Highlights

- As school leaders, we must begin with the end of our leadership in mind. Developing a succession plan *before* a leadership change will help schools transition effectively and avoid the pitfalls that often come with such a change.

- Schools need a combination of Rockstars and Superstars on their staff.

CONCLUSION

As we wrap up this book, we want to reiterate what we shared in our introduction. We are not here to tell you that we have all the answers or that the work is easy. We wrote this book because, as school leaders, each one of us had to figure out on our own how to operationalize best leadership practices.

Administrator Clarity is about what you expect your teachers to do and how their work impacts student learning. It is not optional. Holding your teachers accountable and showing them their efficacy is not an exercise in control; it is an exercise in empowerment.

We are imperfect leaders, leading every single day and doing our best to figure it all out. Sometimes we succeed wildly, and at other times we learn from our failures. What we have compiled here is our best version of some of the things we have figured out along the way.

What we know for certain is that our roles matter. Being a leader who leads with Administrator Clarity is critical in the ever-changing landscape of our profession.

We know and believe that intentional leaders hold their staff accountable to the high standards that their students deserve. When they do this, those staff members in turn hold one another accountable to a culture of clarity. When this happens, collective efficacy is reinforced, and students are the winners.

APPENDIX

Administrator Clarity Self-Assessment

Rate yourself on a scale of 1 to 5 in the following domains: purpose, implementation, communication, and sustainability.

5: Strongly agree (all day, every day)

4: Mostly true of my actions and behaviors (evident most days)

3: Somewhat true of my actions and behaviors (evident on some days)

2: Not very true of my actions and behaviors (*yet*) (evident sometimes but also unclear)

1: Not true of my actions and behaviors

Purpose

Characteristics	Self-Assessment Score
I have worked with my school-based leadership team on our school mission and vision and elicited their feedback on our direction and core values.	
I am self-actualized and work to recognize and name my biases and prejudices so that it does not interfere with my work.	
I engage in activities that build or improve my leadership abilities.	
I am on a constant journey of self-improvement.	
I can deliver an elevator speech that clearly and succinctly describes the purpose and goals embraced by all members of my school community.	
I work with my staff to co-construct and regularly revisit school-wide norms, so that these are inclusive of all stakeholders on my campus.	
Total score =	
Total score ÷ Number of questions =	

Implementation

Characteristics	Self-Assessment Score
I have worked tirelessly to articulate goals at my school and to create systems that support these goals.	
If you look at my school's budget, you would be able to name two or three of the goals that the school is working toward.	
I have strategically allocated my time in such a way that the vast majority of my days are spent working on things that directly align with my school's goals.	
When I plan or facilitate professional development with staff, nearly all of it aligns with the school's goals.	
Total score =	
Total score ÷ Number of questions =	

Communication

Characteristics	Self-Assessment Score
I approach situations with compassionate curiosity by listening with empathy, asking questions to understand, and viewing behavior as communication.	
I orient toward optimism and consider how I share and celebrate successes, acknowledge the effort and accomplishments of others, and express gratitude.	
I seek to strike a balance between supportive encouragement and critical feedback for all community members.	
Stakeholders come to me unprompted for support and to share successes.	
I interact informally with students, staff, and families throughout the day.	
I feel that I truly know the members on my school staff and care deeply for them.	
I am not afraid to have hard conversations when the conversations need to happen.	
Total score =	
Total score ÷ Number of questions =	

Sustainability

Characteristics	Self-Assessment Score
I publicly acknowledge the work of staff to celebrate the learning process, focusing on exemplars and works in progress.	
I establish balance and boundaries by asking for help, saying no when necessary, delegating, and embracing shared leadership.	
I solicit feedback from various stakeholders on my approach to leadership, my actions and impact, and my ability to model leadership competencies.	
I advocate for myself, ask for support when needed, and seek out resources to further my understanding and develop my skills.	
Total score =	
Total score ÷ Number of questions =	

Administrator Clarity
Staff Assessment

Confidentially, rate your administrator on a scale of 1 to 5 in the following domains.

5: Strongly agree (all day, every day)

4: Mostly true of my actions and behaviors (evident most days)

3: Somewhat true of my actions and behaviors (evident on some days)

2: Not very true of my actions and behaviors (*yet*) (evident sometimes but also unclear)

1: Not true of my actions and behaviors

Purpose

Characteristics	Assessment Score
Administrator has worked with my school-based leadership team on our school mission and vision, and elicited their feedback on our direction and core values.	
Administrator is aware of their attitudes, values, biases, and prejudices.	
Administrator seems to engage in activities that build or improve their leadership abilities.	
Administrator is always looking to improve.	
Administrator can articulate clearly and succinctly the purpose and goals embraced by all members of our school community.	
Administrator co-constructs and regularly revisits school-wide norms, ensuring that they incorporate the views, concerns, and aspirations of staff, students, and families.	
Total score =	
Total score ÷ Number of questions =	

Implementation

Characteristics	Assessment Score
Administrator has worked to articulate goals at the school and to create systems that support these goals.	
If you look at my school's budget, you would be able to name two or three of the goals the school is working toward.	
Administrator seems to allocate their time in such a way that the vast majority of the day is spent working on things that directly align with the school's goals.	
When administrator plans or facilitates professional development with staff, nearly all of it aligns with the school's goals.	
Total score =	
Total score ÷ Number of questions =	

Communication

Characteristics	Assessment Score
Administrator approaches situations with compassionate curiosity by listening with empathy, asking questions to understand, and viewing behavior as communication.	
Administrator orients toward optimism and shares and celebrates successes, acknowledges the effort and accomplishments of others, and expresses gratitude.	
Administrator seeks to strike a balance between supportive encouragement and critical feedback for all community members.	
Stakeholders can go to administrator unprompted for support and will be supported.	
Administrator interacts informally with students, staff, and families throughout the day.	
I feel that administrator truly knows the members of our school staff and cares deeply for them.	
Administrator is able to approach challenging conversations to move the school forward.	
Total score =	
Total score ÷ Number of questions =	

Sustainability

Characteristics	Self-Assessment Score
Administrator publicly acknowledges the work of staff to celebrate the learning process, focusing on examples and works in progress.	
Administrator establishes balance and boundaries by asking for help, saying no when necessary, delegating, and embracing shared leadership.	
Administrator solicits feedback from various stakeholders on their approach to leadership, actions and impact, and ability to model leadership competencies.	
Administrator advocates for self, asks for support when needed, and seeks out resources to further their understanding and develop my skills.	
Administrator supports colleagues and leverages their expertise when challenges arise.	
Administrator expresses appreciation for students, staff, and families, both publicly and privately.	

Total score =

Total score ÷ Number of questions =

Administrator Clarity Planning Guide

Jot down specific actions of Administrator Clarity you commit to implementing.

Domain: Purpose	Domain: Implementation

Domain: Communication	Domain: Sustainability

A Peek at the Week

Identify important meetings, school or district events, and celebrations going on throughout the week that impact your staff. Add them to a weekly calendar and share with staff before the start of the week.

Monday	Tuesday	Wednesday	Thursday	Friday

Articulating Your "Why"

What is your purpose, cause, or belief?	
Why does your school exist?	
Why do you get out of bed every morning?	
Why should anyone care?	

Reflective Communication— Identifying a "Why" Statement

Question	Response
What is your purpose, cause, or belief?	My purpose is:
Why does your school exist?	My school exists because:
Why do you get out of bed every morning?	I get out of bed every morning to/because:

Why should anyone care?	We should care because:

Write down your "why" statement.

Now reread it and shorten your "why" statement by taking out five words.

Reread it and hone in on important phrases and words. Make your "why" statement ten or fewer words. Focus and be intentional with your word choice.

Physical Communication—Remember Your "Why" Bulletin Board

1. Have staff members think about their "why."

2. Ask them to write down one word that embodies their "why" (e.g., "passion," "motivation," "impact").

3. Have staff members turn and talk to share their one "why" word and explain the rationale for choosing that word to embody their "why."

4. Display the words on a staff bulletin board for everyone in the community to see.

Personal Communication— Remember Your "Why" Notes

Being vulnerable with your staff is important. When you can authentically share something with your staff that helps you strengthen your "why" for being in education, you are modeling for them to do the same. It can be something that has happened in the past, something that happened today, or something you hope for in the future.

Instructional Communication—
Informal Observations
with Your "Why"

Here is a template for observation notes with "why."

Our "why"	[Type "why" here.]
The connection	[Write observations that connect with the "why" that was observed during the walk-through.]

Core Values Questions

Question	Response
What forms the foundation on which you work?	_____ forms the foundation on which I work because _____ .
What is a constant in the ever-changing world of your school?	A constant in the ever-changing world of my school is _____ .
How do you interact with one another?	We interact with one another by _____ .
Which strategies will you use to employ your mission?	I will use _____ strategies to employ our mission.
What are the basic elements of how you go about your work? What are the practices you use in everything you do?	I go about my work by _____ . The practices I use in everything I do are _____ .

Examples of School Mission, Vision, and Core Values

Mission	Vision	Core Values
School A		
ABC Elementary School is committed to growing the hearts, minds, and bodies of all students through robust academic, social-emotional, and physical education that develops the whole child.	ABC Elementary School prepares and motivates our students for a rapidly changing world by instilling in them critical thinking skills and a global perspective. Students will have success for today and be prepared for tomorrow.	• Honesty, loyalty • Perseverance • Compassion
School B		
Dynamic Learning Academy is dedicated to educating confident, lifelong learners by providing academic rigor, ensuring a dynamic and inclusive learning environment, and providing flexible and innovative learning.	At Dynamic Learning Academy, we leave an everlasting fingerprint on the greater community by ensuring our students are capable of reaching their goals and dreams.	• Flexibility • Inclusiveness • Relationships • Accountability • Innovation • Respect • Iteration • Integrity
School C		
Our school is devoted to maximizing student achievement and nurturing individual talent.	We partner with families and the community to create an environment where personal development and academic growth are our cornerstones. We create global citizens.	• Respect • Collaboration • High expectations • Responsibility • Equity • Pride

Mission	Vision	Core Values
School D		
Sparky Middle School staff are dedicated to modeling and developing character, responsibility, and high achievement.	Sparky Middle School provides educational opportunities that will inspire all students to evolve into successful twenty-first-century learners.	• Achievement • Character • Responsibility

Sample Needs Assessment

Look at the data. What are some things that jump out at you? List facts only.

What can you celebrate? Be specific.

For this next section, look closely at one subject area at a time.

What is the percentage of **all** students meeting or exceeding proficiency in each content area?	What is the percentage of previously identified specific student groups meeting or exceeding proficiency in each content area?	Are there gaps in achievement between certain groups and all students? What are these gaps?
Which specific domains or skills did most students meet or exceed proficiency with?	Which specific domains or skills did these student groups meet or exceed proficiency with?	Are there gaps in achievement in these specific domains or skills between certain groups and all students? What are these gaps?

Which specific domains or skills did most students struggle the most with?	Which specific domains or skills did certain student groups struggle the most with?	Are there gaps in achievement in these domains or skills between certain groups and all students? What are these gaps?
List **possible** school-related barriers impacting the achievement gap between student groups.		
List **possible** school-related strategies that will positively impact the achievement gap between student groups.		
Identify three strategies from this list that are evidenced based and can yield results.		
Identify one strategy from this list that can be implemented with fidelity during the coming school year.		
Identify a specific domain or skill area that is high leverage and needed among (1) all students and/ or (2) specific student groups.		

Typical Administrator versus Administrator with Clarity

A Typical Administrator	An Administrator Who Leads with Administrator Clarity	What This Sounds Like in Practice	Your Turn (Think of a time when you can practice this aspect of intentional leadership, and make a note in this space.)
Drives teachers	Coaches teachers	"I was excited to see you take a risk and try ___."	
Relies on authority	Relies on goodwill	"I believe each of you comes here every day to do the best you can, and I want to remove barriers so that you may achieve that goal."	
Generates fear	Inspires enthusiasm	"We are all in this together. I am your number one cheerleader and will have your back as we move forward."	
Says "I" and "my"	Says "we" and "our"	"We are doing great things for our school and our students."	
Directs people	Develops people	"I appreciate how this team is working toward our school goal of _____."	
Takes credit	Gives credit	"This school's success is a result of the hard work of every member of this school team. You all make me proud of our profession."	

A Typical Administrator	An Administrator Who Leads with Administrator Clarity	What This Sounds Like in Practice	Your Turn (Think of a time when you can practice this aspect of intentional leadership, and make a note in this space.)
Says "Go"	Says "Let's go"	"I know this is a challenging goal, but I believe that working together and with support from me every step of the way, we can get there."	
Focuses on output	Focuses on process	"Let's not worry yet about the end result; let's focus on each step, one day at a time, while we work toward our goal."	
Shares goals	Shares why	"This isn't about **what** we are going to do as a school; it's about **why** what we do, day in and day out, matters to all of us."	
Craves perfection	Celebrates progress	"We may not be there **yet**, but I see us making significant progress every step of the way, and I applaud the efforts being put forth by our team."	
Gives solutions	Solicits feedback	"Rather than my telling you how I want it done, why don't you tell me your ideas on ways _____ could be more effective."	

Ways to Communicate School Goals with Stakeholders

Communication Purpose and Frequency	Check When Complete
Weekly Keep your school-wide goals at the top of every school site meeting agenda.	
Monthly Highlight the goals in your newsletter to the school community. (Summarize the rationale for the goals based on the needs assessment—in other words, share your data! Transparency is critical.)	
Monthly Highlight the goals in your staff newsletter. It's a great idea to have a section showcasing the area of focus at the top of the newsletter.	
Monthly Highlight which goals are being addressed in your yearlong school improvement plan and how you are allocating resources and professional development aligned with these goals.	
Quarterly Share progress toward goals with everyone involved.	
Annually Share the summary of results for all goals.	

Long-Range Plan Aligned with Funding Sources

Site Goal #1

Action Steps	Funding Source and Amount	Evidence	Resources	Time Line
What action steps will we take to make progress toward our goal?	*What funding will be needed to support the actions?*	*What evidence will we use to measure progress?*	*What are the best resources?*	*What is an appropriate time line for the action steps?*

Site Goal #2

Action Steps	Funding Source and Amount	Evidence	Resources	Time Line
What action steps will we take to make progress toward our goal?	*What funding will be needed to support the actions?*	*What evidence will we use to measure progress?*	*What are the best resources?*	*What is an appropriate time line for the action steps?*

Site Goal #3

Action Steps	Funding Source and Amount	Evidence	Resources	Time Line
What action steps will we take to make progress toward our goal?	*What funding will be needed to support the actions?*	*What evidence will we use to measure progress?*	*What are the best resources?*	*What is an appropriate time line for the action steps?*

Leading with **ADMINISTRATOR CLARITY**

REFERENCES

Allensworth, Elaine M., and Holly Hart. "How Do Principals Influence Student Achievement?" Chicago, IL: University of Chicago Consortium on School. Last updated June 2018. https://consortium.uchicago.edu/sites/default/files/2018-10/Leadership%20Snapshot-Mar2018-Consortium.pdf.

Ata, Sinan. "Rockstars vs Superstars—Get to Know Your People." *Medium*. July 23, 2019. https://sinanata.medium.com/rockstars-vs-superstars-get-to-know-your-people-b30cd878e0a1.

Blase, Jo, Joseph Blase, and Dana Yon Phillips. *Handbook of School Improvement: How High-Performing Principals Create High-Performing Schools*. Thousand Oaks, CA: Corwin, 2010.

Every Student Succeeds Act, 20 U.S.C. § 6301 (2015). congress.gov/114/plaws/publ95/PLAW-114publ95.pdf.

Garmston, Robert J. "Collaborative Culture: Raise the Level of Conversation by Using Paraphrasing as a Listening Skill," *Journal of Staff Development* 29, no. 2 (Spring 2008).

Grissom, Jason A., Anna J. Egalite, and Constance A. Lindsay. 2021. "How Principals Affect Students and Schools: A Systematic Synthesis of Two Decades of Research." New York: The Wallace Foundation.

Grissom, Jason A., and Susanna Loeb. "Triangulating Principal Effectiveness: How Perspectives of Parents, Teachers, and Assistant Principals Identify the Central Importance of Managerial Skills." National Center for Analysis of Longitudinal Data in Education Research. Washington, DC: Urban Institute, October 1, 2011. https://www.urban.org/sites/default/files/publication/33316/1001443-Triangulating-Principal-Effectiveness-How-Perspectives-of-Parents-Teachers-and-Assistant-Principals-Identify-the-Central-Importance-of-Managerial-Skills.PDF.

Hargie, Owen. *Skilled Interpersonal Communication: Research, Theory and Practice*. Oxfordshire, UK: Routledge, 2021.

Harper, Amelia. "Principal: Listening to, Caring for Staff's Needs Key to Success." K–12 Dive. January 4, 2019. https://www.k12dive.com/news/principal-listening-to-caring-for-staffs-needs-key-to-success/545197.

Hattie, John. Visible Learning for Teachers: Maximizing Impact on Learning. London: Routledge, 2012.

Hattie, John. "Collective Teacher Efficacy (CTE) According to John Hattie." *Visible Learning*. Last updated October 12, 2018. https://visible-learning.org/2018/03/collective-teacher-efficacy-hattie.

Horng, Eileen Lai, Daniel Klasik, and Susanna Loeb. "Principal's Time Use and School Effectiveness." *American Journal of Education* 116, no. 4 (2010): 491–523. https://www.jstor.org/stable/10.1086/653625.

Jackson, Laura. "The Truth about Teacher Recognition: How to Get It and Give It." TaraTeachers.com. January 21, 2022. https://www.taraedtech.com/blog/teacher-recognition-post

Johnson, Christopher. "Leaders Who Authentically Embrace Diversity, Equity & Inclusion Believe These 8 Things." Nonprofit Leadership Center. February 22, 2021. https://nlctb.org/tips/inclusive-leadership.

Ladd, Helen. "Teachers' Perceptions of Their Working Conditions: How Predictive of Policy-Relevant Outcomes?" National Center for Analysis of Longitudinal Data in Education Research. Washington, DC: Urban Institute, 2009. https://caldercenter.org/publications/teachers-perceptions-their-working -conditions-how-predictive-policy-relevant-outcomes.

Lewis, Tom D., and Gerald Graham. "7 Tips for Effective Listening: Productive Listening Does Not Occur Naturally. It Requires Hard Work and Practice." Internal Auditor, August 2003. https://link.gale.com/apps/doc/A106863366 /AONE?u=anon~48509cb7&sid=googleScholar&xid=12f0aec2.

Leithwood, Kenneth, Karen Seashore Louis, Stephen Anderson, and Kyla Wahlstrom. "Review of Research: How Leadership Influences Student Learning." New York: Wallace Foundation, 2004.

Louis, Karen Seashore, Kenneth Leithwood, Kyla L. Wahlstrom, Stephen E. Anderson, et al. "Learning from Leadership: Investigating the Links to Improved Student Learning." University of Minnesota, Center for Applied Research and Educational Improvement, and University of Toronto, Ontario Institute for Studies in Education. July 2010. https://www.wallacefoundation .org/knowledge-center/Documents/Investigating-the-Links-to-Improved -Student-Learning.pdf.

McKeown, Dave. "9 Alternative Ways to Lead with Authenticity." *Inc.* March 7, 2019. https://www.inc.com/dave-mckeown/9-unique-ways-to-lead-with -authenticity.html.

Mello, Tommy. "Keep Changing Your Mind? According to Jeff Bezos, That's a Sign of High Intelligence." *Inc.* May 6, 2019. https://www.inc.com/tommy-mello /keep-changing-your-mind-according-to-jeff-bezos-thats-a-sign-of-high -intelligence.html.

National Association of Secondary School Principals and National Association of Elementary School Principals. "Leadership Matters: What the Research Says about the Importance of Principal Leadership." Reston, VA: National Association of Secondary School Principals and National Association of Elementary School Principals, 2013. https://www.naesp.org/sites/default /files/LeadershipMatters.pdf.

Rice, Jennifer King. "Principal Effectiveness and Leadership in an Era of Accountability: What Research Says National Center for Analysis of Longitudinal Data in Education Research. Washington, DC: Urban Institute, April 2010. https://files.eric.ed.gov/fulltext/ED509682.pdf.

Sinek, Simon. "What Diversity & Inclusion Is Really About." YouTube Video. December 16, 2020. https://www.youtube.com/watch?v=XisFCRrQivU.

Sinek, Simon. *Start with Why: How Great Leaders Inspire Everyone to Take Action*. Harlow, England: Penguin Books, 2011.

Slide, Frank. "What Are the Five Performance Objectives of Operations Management?" *Frank Slide* (blog). Last accessed February 1, 2022, https://www.frankslide.com/what-are-the-five-performance-objectives-of -operations-management.

Wiseman, Liz, and Greg McKeown. Multipliers: How the Best Leaders Make Everyone Smarter. New York: HarperBusiness, 2010.

Wooden, John. "John Wooden Quotes on Leadership." Last accessed March 11, 2022. https://johnlutz.com/uplifting-quotes/john-wooden.

ACKNOWLEDGMENTS

Writing this book was the amalgamation of learning from many amazing mentors, who left an indelible print on my heart. To Dr. Christine Hamlin, who taught me to lead with grace and compassion. Dr. Isa DeArmas, who modeled student-first leadership. Tim Forson, whose integrity was inspiring. Susan Bender, who helped me find the "prettier" side of things. To my CIP, Carin and Marine, colleagues once, friends forever. To all that I have had the joy of mentoring, may you always know your impact! To my husband, Brian, and my supportive family, you all are my everything.

— **Sandy Brunet**

As an educator, I strive to continuously lead through and with the connections and relationships I've made with so many people who are part of my journey. To my third grade teacher, who helped me feel seen; to my dearest friends, who encourage me with daily optimism; to the many brave mentors, who opened new doors for me and saw talents I didn't quite see in myself; to my original CIP: Sandy and Marine, who give me space to be brave and authentic; and, of course, to Jeff and my family for being the best support system anyone could ever have.

— **Carin Fractor**

I am so grateful to have been given an opportunity to write a book with my coalition of intentional peers, Carin and Sandy. Taking our passions and being able to collaborate on something we're all so invested in has been a dream come true. Thank you to my parents for always believing in my goals; thank you to my sister for her constant advice and support; and, of course, thank you to my husband, who is always there for me and knows just what to say. Finally, thank you to my two sons, Jake and Josh. You are my everything.

— **Marine Freibrun**

ABOUT THE AUTHORS

Sandy Brunet is a school administrator with over fifteen years' experience leading schools in California, Hawaii, and Florida. Her educational leadership experiences include roles in public brick-and-mortar schools, virtual charter schools, and hybrid blended learning schools. Sandy has been recognized for her collaborative efforts to transform school culture by building positive relationships and increasing school achievement. She holds a master's degree in educational administration and a bachelor's degree in communication studies from UCLA. When she isn't knee-deep in school leadership, she enjoys spending time with her husband, Brain, and her two sons, Caden and JT, in their North Florida community.

Carin Fractor is a district administrator with over twenty years' experience in public education. Her experiences range from paraeducator, classroom teacher, and instructional coach to school site administrator, district leader, and mom to two elementary-age children. She leads with the mindset that each person with whom she works should feel valued. Carin holds a doctorate degree in education from the University of Southern California as well as a master's degree in educational administration from California State University, Northridge. She resides in Southern California with her family, and can often be found jet-setting around the globe with her family or at home, enjoying a day with absolutely no schedule at all.

Marine Freibrun is an elementary educator with over twelve years' experience as a classroom teacher, instructional coach, PBIS coordinator, and assessment coordinator for the Idaho State Department of Education. She is also the educational content creator behind Tales from a Very Busy Teacher. She creates, shares, and presents effective strategies to an audience of over 130,000 educators on Instagram and Facebook. She is also the author of *Getting Started with Teacher Clarity*. She holds a master's degree in educational leadership from California State University, Northridge. She resides with her husband and two boys in Idaho, where they enjoy family time outdoors.